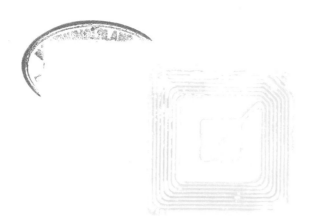

A DECADE OF
RIBA STUDENT COMPETITIONS

Peter Krespi, Architectural Association, UK, Commended 1985

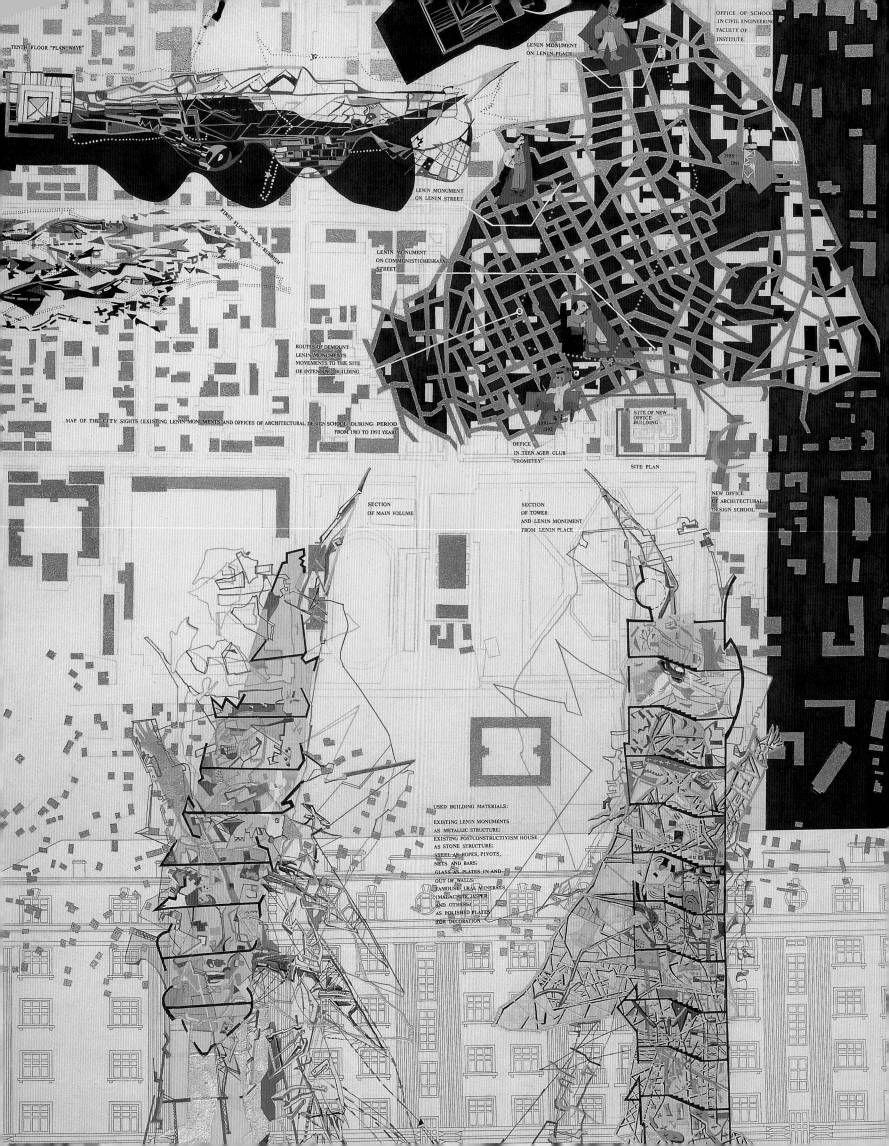

TENTH FLOOR "PLAN-WAVE"

OFFICE OF SCHOOL
IN CIVIL ENGINEERING
FACULTY OF
INSTITUTE

LENIN MONUMENT
ON LENIN PLACE

1988-
1991

LENIN MONUMENT
ON LENIN STREET

FIRST FLOOR "PLAN-RUBBISH"

LENIN MONUMENT
ON COMMUNISTICHESKAYA
STREET

ROUTES OF DEMOUNT
LENIN MONUMENTS
MOVEMENTS TO THE SITE
OF INTENDING BUILDING

SITE OF NEW
OFFICE
BUILDING

1991-
1992

MAP OF THE CITY SIGHTS (EXISTING LENIN MONUMENTS AND OFFICES OF ARCHITECTURAL DESIGN SCHOOL DURING PERIOD
FROM 1983 TO 1992 YEAR)

OFFICE
IN TEEN AGER CLUB
"PROMETEY"

SITE PLAN

SECTION
OF MAIN VOLUME

SECTION
OF TOWER
AND LENIN MONUMENT
FROM LENIN PLACE

NEW OFFICE
OF ARCHITECTURAL
DESIGN SCHOOL

USED BUILDING MATERIALS:

EXISTING LENIN MONUMENTS
AS METALLIC STRUCTURE;
EXISTING POSTCONSTRUCTIVISM HOUSE
AS STONE STRUCTURE;
STEEL AS ROPES, PIVOTS,
NETS AND BARS;
GLASS AS PLATES IN AND
OUT OF WALLS;
FAMOUSE URAL MINERALS
(MALACHITE, JASPER
AND OTHERS)
AS POLISHED PLATES
FOR DECORATION

International Union of Architects
JOURNAL OF ARCHITECTURAL THEORY AND CRITICISM

EDITOR: Jorge Glusberg   PUBLISHER: Andreas Papadakis

A DECADE OF
RIBA STUDENT COMPETITIONS

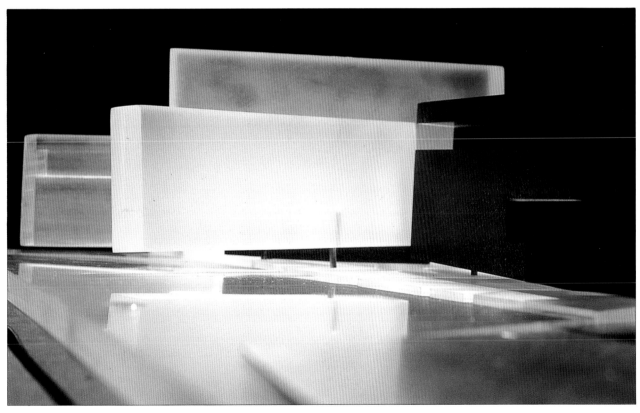

ABOVE: Zaha Hadid, Media Park, Zollhof 3, Judge 1992
OPPOSITE: Nataliya Maximova, Dilara Zinatulina, Svetlana Nasretdinova, Svetlana Rasuleva et al,
Sultana House, Regional Design School, Bashkirsky Dom, Russia, Joint 3rd Prize 1992

ACADEMY EDITIONS•LONDON

Acknowledgements

The Editor and Publisher are grateful to the architects and students who have supplied material for this issue and to Eugenie Biddle of the RIBA for her much appreciated assistance and cooperation. Front cover: Catalin Mihai Dragomir, 'Theories of Meaning', Bartlett School of Architecture, UK, Commended 1992; Back cover: Itsuko Hasegawa, Busshoji Elementary School, Japan, Judge 1992; Inside covers: Christine Hawley with Paul Cook, World Trade Centre, Berlin, Judge 1992. Photo credits: p32 John Donat; p49 Paul Bricknell.

I am delighted that Jorge Glusberg, Andreas Papadakis and the UIA have joined us in celebrating this exciting moment – the Tenth Anniversary of the RIBA International Competition for Students of Architecture. This fascinating publication not only marks the anniversary, but is a tribute to the achievements of the judges and the new generations of architects worldwide. The present and the future look promising.

Richard McCormac

EDITOR: Jorge Glusberg PUBLISHER: Andreas Papadakis

EDITORIAL BOARD
Oriol Bohigas, Mario Botta, Nils Carlson, Henri Ciriani, Charles Correa, Tomás Dagnino, Francesco Dal Co, Rafael dela Hoz, Sverre Fehn, Kenneth Frampton, Vittorio Gregotti, Rod Hackney, Hans Hollein, Arata Isozaki, Philip Johnson, Josef Kleihues, Heinrich Klotz, Richard Meier, Pierluigi Nicolin, Georgi Stoilov

EDITORIAL TEAM: Maggie Toy, Natasha Robertson, COORDINATOR: Diego Forero, DESIGNER: Mario Bettela

Edited by Jorge Glusberg at the CAYC (Centre for Art and Communication) foundation, Elpidio Gonzalez 4070, (1407) Buenos Aires, Argentina
Published on behalf of the International Union of Architects by the Academy Group Ltd, 42 Leinster Gardens, London W2 3AN
ISSN: 0953 220X

First published in Great Britain in 1992 by Academy Editions, an imprint of the
ACADEMY GROUP LTD, 42 LEINSTER GARDENS, LONDON W2 3AN
A member of the VCH Publishing Group
ISBN: 1-85490-1370 PB (UK)

Distributed to the trade in the United States of America by
ST MARTIN'S PRESS, 175 FIFTH AVENUE, NEW YORK, NY 10010
ISBN: 0-312-07894-3 (USA)

Printed and bound in Singapore

Contents

Tadao Ando, JR Kyoto Station, Judge 1989

A DECADE OF
RIBA STUDENT COMPETITIONS

PETER COOK
THE INTERNATIONAL COMPETITION

Since almost every human activity that involves people and initiative also implies the competitive instinct, it should come as no surprise that architects too resort to such overt and even aggressive operations as holding competitions. To encourage students to compete, openly, independently and on a world stage is merely underscoring the point.

In parallel, we can look at the whole business of architecture as a culture in its own right. How does it really lurch from mode to mode, from love to hate, from reality to abstraction, from easy recognition to obscurity?

There must have been a time when students per se were shadowy creatures, at best the factotum of the Master Architect, but more likely, a discreet follower, pupil or assistant who just might grow into a reasonable reproduction of his master one day.

You will note, that so far I have kept the conversation well in the male gender, and have not mentioned any of the institutions that are now considered central to this history, such as architecture schools, magazines, books, teachers, gurus, printing, travel.

It is just so.

The history of the International Student Competition that has for ten years been run by the RIBA in London, and it is very much an international event, is a mirror and a product of the history of the emancipation of architecture as a study. So that the rescue of the young man and later the young woman from the clutches of an opportunist (or even a benevolent) senior architect, became an essential. Similarly, we can see the idea of a free-for-all competition as another way of rescue. For after a while, institutions of learning can themselves start to reproduce all the vagaries and psychological warfare that occur within families and within offices. The master architect becomes the oppressive, or arrogant, or simply rather bright teacher. At a certain moment the student might think, 'yes, yes, but what I want to do is this'.

The magazine has the same role, nobody can intercept it coming through your door, and, except in poor and very repressed places, librarians don't know enough about architecture to tell the difference between a common-place editorial and something really hot.

So the competition and the circulation of ideas do start to develop together, it becomes possible for a student with an interesting idea or with overt talent to bypass the limitations of the local discussion and edge forward. Suddenly in the pages of the publication or on the wall of the gallery, he sees that someone else, someone with a very odd name and a curious style of drawing has been thinking along similar lines. Or he notices that the way Lithuanians do roofs is really weird, but rather good.

In Scandinavia and Germany the competitions system is highly developed as the route through which young architects force themselves upon the building scene and older architects jostle with each other to get the big commissions. This leaves open the question of ideas competitions or student competitions, where the result must not be built . . . so maybe need not be buildable. The issue of concept as distinct from construction, idea as part of culture, abstraction as a possible strategy as well as a tactic for thought, at some point in the chain, leads to the pushing forward of architectural boundaries and therefore the pushing forward of the art of architecture itself. Belief in the value of such a chain is not necessarily an avant-gardist position, for there are so many parallels in science, music, economics, literature and art that are readily accepted.

If however, you are a creative architectural academic, you are tempted and fascinated by the forcefulness of parallel streams to that of your own. However wedded one is to the primacy of the 'studio' tradition, to be challenged by another more wayward stream can be exciting. Funny things happen in competitions, there are lurches of belief or interpretation, there are geographic shifts in primacy of ideas or inspiration. For example, Brazil drops out of the scene and Luxembourg emerges, either of them creating an irritation to the architecturally arrogant centres of New York or London who always feel that they are where the conversation is at. If you are a creative academic you are almost as eager as your students to know which way Aldo van Eyck or Zaha Hadid might jump, given a load of student work they don't know. Your own students (and I have fathered both winners and losers of this particular competition) behave curiously, either smothering and losing their ideas by too much cleverness, too many lines, too many private references, or sailing past the others by sheer nerve. Some of the best, of course, are scared by the bunfight aspect of it all, forgetting that their future survival in the world of getting-it-done will be one giant bunfight of an altogether tougher breed.

In theory of course the International Student competition could be used as a roundabout way of influencing the scene: it could have a series of worthy academics or captains of the architectural industry, 'useful contacts' or perpetrators of a particular hard-line, so that it was seen that a set of observances was necessary if you are to become an accredited nice young architect.

None of this.

The founders of the competition were Patrick Hodgkinson, Denis Serjeant and Allen Cunningham. I joined them much later during (I think) the fifth or sixth

Sasa Randic, New Utopia, University of Zagreb, Croatia, 2nd Prize 1989

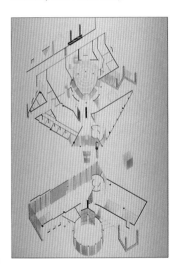

Hrvoje Graso, Vedran Kogl, University of Zagreb, Croatia, Commended 1985

Natalya Maximova, Dilara Zinatulina, Svetlana Nasretdinova, Svetlana Rasaleva et al, Regional Design School, Bashkirsky Dom, Russia, Joint 3rd Prize 1992

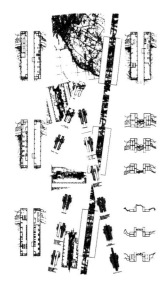

Andrew Birds, Polytechnic of Central London, UK, 1st Prize 1984

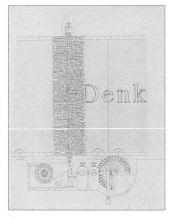

Stephen Harty, No Man's Land, Bartlett School of Architecture, UK, 2nd Prize 1991

Competition period. By this time the thing had a particularly English trajectory as far as its organisation was concerned, but also, by then, it had increasingly international trajectory as far as the architecture was concerned. Discussion about the jurors was very open, almost anybody from the elite band who we can now recognise as winners of the Pritzker prize and Carlsberg Prizes through to some scruffy herbert who just about made it to the faculty of an obscure school of architecture and is a hero in pub circles. Since it is England, there is of course much furrowing of brows over sponsorship and logistics mixed with the fascinating mixture of kindness, benigness and oil tanker-like dexterity of the RIBA as an institution. That loved and hated institution of the Royal Academy has also emerged as the natural place for such work to be displayed.

As I write, strenuous efforts are being made to put the exhibition of winning projects on the road. For it to be truly international it must be viewable internationally. This is the first book of the competition, at last we can see the pattern of movement and the feel of interaction between formed architects and architecture with that which is forming.

Patrick Hodgkinson has been tireless and full of wheezes that might get someone on board here, someone subscribing there, someone pulling in someone there. The late Denis Serjeant was also in the greatest tradition of the English wise enthusiast. He was the youngest of us all and I have no doubt that the whole notion of a young exhibition was central to his motivation. His school at Cheltenham must have been a marvellous, zany place. So that part of my own reputation that comes under the 'fast and loose' category of pigeonholing was obviously the reason why they felt that I could help. Lest it all sound like a version of the English schoolboy prank turned into an intellectual game, we must remember that Allen Cunningham has been there all along, up to the present day. He is the creative cynic amongst us, fearful of bias, fearful of the vagaries of the world where people do or do not do things. But he himself is another dooer, who made much of the exhibiting and publishing and the basic happening of the thing possible. He has usually been the one who has suggested the more serious and rational names to be brought over as jurors.

Wiggins Teape the paper people, sponsored the first competition in 1983. Eldred Evans and her partner David Shalev were the judges. At that point there were 75 entries from 42 schools in only three countries. Strong, clear architects, limited publicity and still a somewhat 'local' air did not prevent it from being a good competition, but the cultural rejuvenation of Regent's Park has the feel of a period in which all seemed fairly well with the world: the inspiration being the Evans & Shalev track record as competition winners themselves. So in the first five years the first prize winning list runs: Bartlett – PCL – AA – Bath – AA; certainly a British-looking path. But already by the second year, Cape Town and Dublin were edging in just behind and by the fifth, the USSR, Israel and Germany were there. Since that time the First Prizes have been distributed among Queensland, Natal, Taiwan, New York and Madrid.

At another time I myself took part in a competition jury alongside Robert Stern. There is almost no point on the architectural scale of taste where you could put us both at the same time. But over the day that ensued, we found ourselves agreeing on every piece of work, on every decision. It happened many times. The competing students might read the issue as 'Ando's year' or 'Rogers' year' but there is a perverse way in which the available talent rises to the top. Certainly in the tenth year, the team of Hasegawa, Hadid and Hawley came back with characteristically straight reporting: 'lots of crap' . . . 'we agreed on the good stuff' . . . 'the winner was clear to us all'. Probably not a scheme entirely to their taste.

Sometimes there is an atmosphere to a competition, the 'gasstop' year for example, led to a higher than usual participation by younger students with only one architect on the panel and a bias towards cheerful technology. It had the historical role of diverting things away from the calm world of rooms or the pre-occupation with the City that attracts so many jurors. For every year it is their choice. The subject is proposed by one judge and thrown around to the others. Almost every time, it is tweaked or even threatened by a piece of very good work that does not answer the brief but is simply brilliant. Some of us believe, even, that the trick is to make every good student feel that the scheme that he or she has sitting in the head is just the right thing for this year's contest. Certainly the themes revolve around the pre-occupations of the urbanised elite of the temperate zone: cultural rejuvenation . . . electronics . . . painting and sculpture . . . animals . . . public buildings and older setting . . . fuelling . . . cities . . . theatre . . . the monument . . . layering. Along with this has come a far higher level of graphic representation than could have been imagined ten years ago.

Ideas are moving around faster. The judges themselves are physically visible in the cities that the competitors come from, publications are more scathing about scruffy and unreadable drawings. The idea of the copy, the facsimile, the digitalised image, virtual reality and the possibility of the impossible have all become the discussion of the age. 'Craft' exists as a curious bedfellow of the effortless simulation. But in the end there are those four sheets of (presumably) paper, seen in a quizzical and impoverished city several weeks later: 'What's this guy trying to tell us' . . . 'Another stripey one' . . . '*must* be Cooper Union' . . . 'hey, this one's *weird* '.

One of the judges that hasn't yet been thought of, but serves as a beautiful example (but since he hasn't been thought of is also a safe example) can tell a whole story. Neil Denari is a fairly young architect who came out of Texas, via Harvard, New York and teaching at SCI ARC in Los Angeles. He wrote a brilliant little publication on 'Architecture Machines' which became (and still is) a cult document peeping out of the undersides of drawing boards all over the Western world. Already three years ago a certain kind of mechanistic formality with crisp black drawings, flat black shadows and barn topped edifices began to appear. Most adult architects (the boring ones) have still not heard of him. Yet already, a second round of students are drawing like that and borrowing the forms as well as the graphics. Peter Wilson and Lebbeus Woods are two more obvious examples of role models – or perhaps fingertip models. Denari as a judge would give giant signals to the student culture: signal one 'You'd better get the old black ink out along with the circle template, guys' (a boring signal); signal two 'We're getting judges younger, this year, his Pritzker prize is still 20 years off!' (a marginally interesting signal); signal three 'See . . . we're still pulling in the thinking and designing architects to vet this one' (a critical signal); signal four 'Its Neil Denari daddy . . . the one you've never heard of' (a signal that returns us to the discussions that schools of architecture must not be allowed to dominate the debate. They too tend to be exclusive half the time).

Another funny one is the look on the face of the editor of the journal that has agreed to publish the winners, a mixture of puzzlement and relief, 'Do we really have to publish this? What is it?' and 'I didn't know they were into that'. For architectural magazines are always running behind the conversation. They (on average) go wild about someone six years after all the young faculty were quoting them. In a way, it is through inspired imitation of the real key figures that a competition such as ours can nudge the media, as well as the unsuspecting exhibition viewer, into recognising the current state of the art.

The present book is about ebb-and-flow in as much as it can be charted by flat paper. The true state of the art is of course a wing of the society and economy outside. The hopes and fears of student projects are cushioned by the desire to be loved. You draw in a certain way because those around you encourage it. You draw thumbnail sketches/axonometrics/exploded diagrams/men with hats/broken pediments . . . whatever . . . because somebody admired them last time. But none of this can entirely smother the issue of form and placement as both a metaphor for action and as a metaphor for the right to a detached position.

'The scheme' is a selected view of world. Just imagine being confronted, as they were in 1987, with the idea of the new and the old. The European view of this might be expected to fall within the context of the inevitable continuity. After all, however radical we think that we are, some other old radical was sitting in this self-same bar believing himself to be a hell of a radical 50 years before.

It leads to a certain comfortableness concerning change. The American or Australian view might choose to be more cautious and almost certainly more pious. There the old, probably meaning 35 years, is to do with the establishment of heritage and is necessarily a precious commodity. Yet paradoxically the American or Australian view of really old cities is often a healthy down-home critique of their snobbism and health hazards.

Somehow, the organisation of the competition has to be aware of all these forces acting together by using the stiff and slow mechanism of drawings, packages, quick opinions, restricted space of exhibitions and misunderstood language (both verbal and visual). So far, it has suited a transitional period in which architecture has discovered its nerve and the world is generally a safer place; despite the paradox of so few architects being fully employed and the incidence of small civil wars.

Out of this competition can come a new breed of accompanying events. A workshop (initially in London), where the better competitors are brought together to debate their work and produce some more. A travelling version of the show, where it can be used as a focus for more workshops, almost like a travelling academy. More involvement of the judges in the aftermath: taking part in the workshops.

It is curious, isn't it that the very insular British, with their very highly established institution for the betterment of architecture have taken it upon themselves to create a really international facility that has taken a place in architectural education? 50 countries send work, that of the locals being a mere 25 per cent of the entry or less. Many competitors make their way to the academy and peer closely at their rival's technique. Those from sleepy and obscure schools know that there is hope. Adult architects are made to feel suitably uncomfortable.

The list of judges and winners already looks like a hall of fame, but it wouldn't matter if that all changed. A year of unknowns doing the judging of unknowns might be great. A development of the competition into a competition-and-workshop might become the model for the next decade. The ranging of the activity with its secretariat remaining in London but its presence elsewhere will also add another dimension.

Ken Grix, Public Baths, Valetta, Malta, University of Bath, UK, 2nd Prize 1987

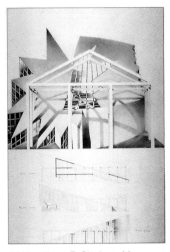

M Korolkov, D Shelest, Moscow Institute of Architecture, Russia, Commended 1985

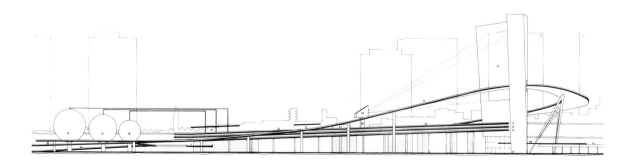

Mark Lecchini, Metropolitan Pitstop, Canterbury College of Art, UK, 1st Prize 1988

1983

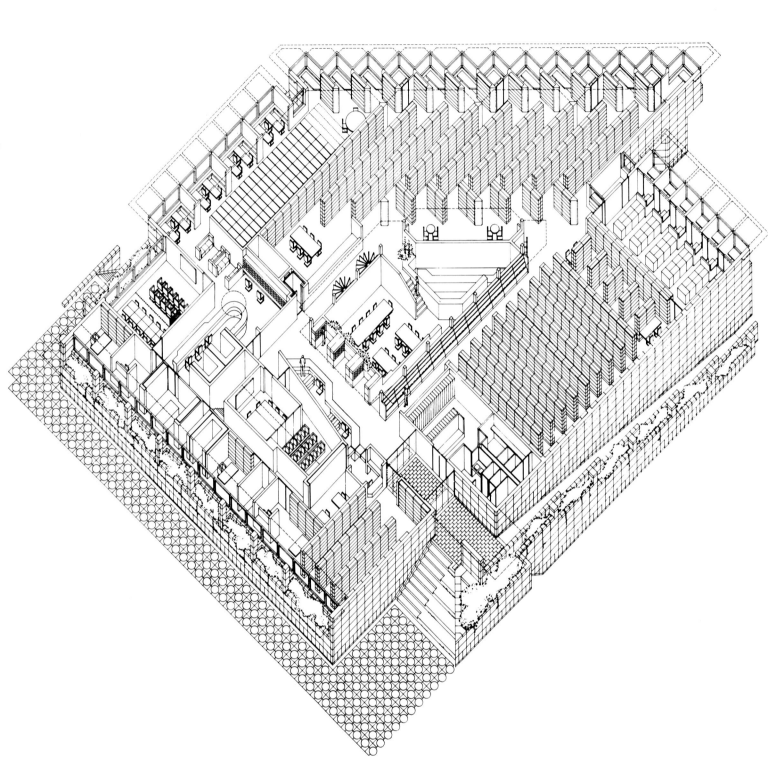

SEVENTH HEAVEN

The competition required entrants to see Regents Park as a collage of six places (Avenue/Promenade; Inner Garden; Lake; Canal; Zoo, and Fields) to which a seventh might be added. Students were encouraged to suggest new routes, planting, etc, but everything that existed was required to be kept intact.

The brief called for a luxury place, which would include a 600-seat restaurant with dancing and banqueting facilities, bars, services, an external protected enclosure capable of holding up to 6,000 people, a bandstand and landscaping. Eldred Evans and David Shalev, who set and assessed the competition, added that the competitors 'may deviate from or add to the brief for good reasons.'

In judging the response to the competition, they wrote: 'We enjoyed the sensitive response to the spirit of the brief, the beautiful drawings which spoke for themselves and the diversity of ideas.

'In broad terms entrants were less concerned with adding another piece to the collage which makes up Regents Park, and more in locating the new facility, either enhancing or underlining an already existing event, discovering a hitherto hidden or invisible relationship, or triggering off an entirely new chain of events.

'Under the first category a favourite theme was to celebrate an entrance, eg from Park Square, from Cumberland Terrace or the church; the north canal basin from Avenue Road/Macclesfield Bridge, from Park Road and from Baker Street; or to formalise an intersection, eg Chester Road and Broadwalk; the top of Broadwalk.

'Under the second and third categories the favourite spot was an area tucked away at the edge of the field enclosure and flanked on two sides by the lake.

'The celebration of an entrance (if not blocking it in the process), the opening up of a new singular axis (if it leads somewhere), a new sequence of events (or string of beads) and the creation of a place as a new focal point are all plausible and useful themes. The better schemes simultaneously explored more than one of them, enriched the diversity of experiences/ spaces in the garden and in addition succeeded in enhancing some of the existing places and creating new relationships between them.'

1st Prize: *Alistair Philip Brierley (below), Bartlett School of Architecture, UK*
2nd Prize: *Gunawan Hartojo, Architectural Association, UK*
3rd Prize: *Yuen Wai Wong, Architectural Association, UK*
Judges: *Eldred Evans, David Shalev (opposite)*

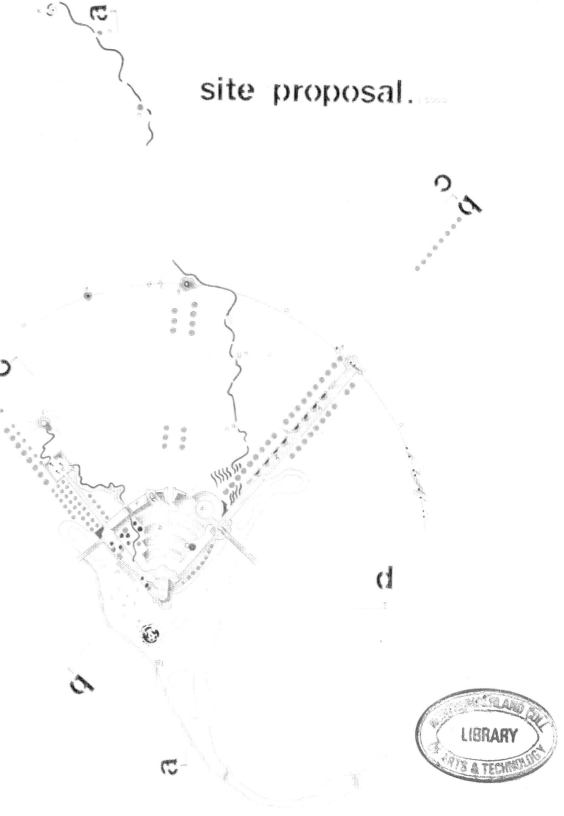

site proposal.

1st PRIZE

*ALISTAIR PHILIP BRIERLEY,
Bartlett School of Architecture,
UK*

This scheme has, with a single stroke and with great economy of means, triggered off an entirely new chain of events. Its beauty is manifold: it unifies the western half of the park including the inner circle, the lake, and the fields creating a complete experience in juxtaposition to Broadwalk. The location of the hub and the routes which it generates naturally respond to the city outside, and the sensitive use of existing elements (bridges, water, trees) together with new elements successfully creates a set of meaningful and inter-related enclosures.

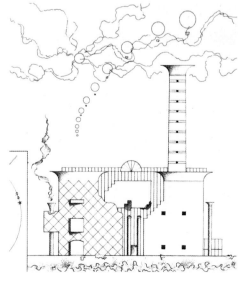

RECENT WORK

ALISTAIR PHILIP BRIERLEY,
St Katharine's Dock Housing
Project

The St Katharine's Dock Housing project comprises 240 residential units (flats, studios, duplexes and houses). All units are contained within a single structure, an L-shaped building continuum wrapping around the north side of the dock. This 'wall' protects and shelters the waterside environment, using the south-facing orientation to utilise the energy-efficient aspects of the scheme. The north side of the wall contains circulation and service spaces, providing an environmental buffer to the dirty and noisy East Smithfield road.

Built form has been generated internally from the programmatic requirements of the residential units, and externally by the site-specific elements of context. As a building following the 'Modern Movement' tradition this is a scheme without superficial 'tack on' decoration, allowing the use of materials to convey the architectural messages. The influence of the residents will provide the colour and life to this flexible backdrop.

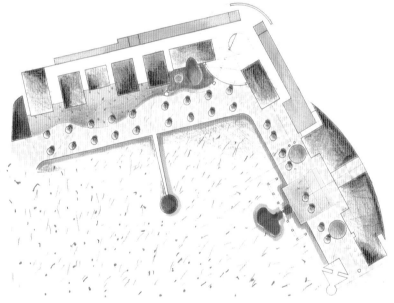

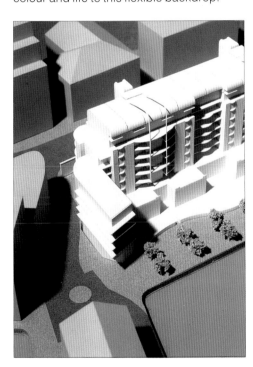

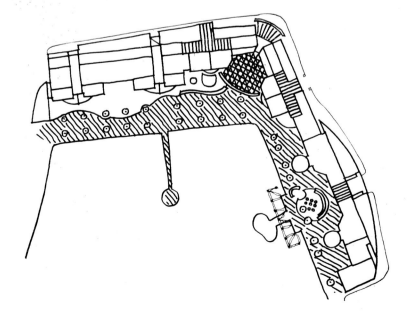

JUDGES
EVANS & SHALEV
Shrivenham Library

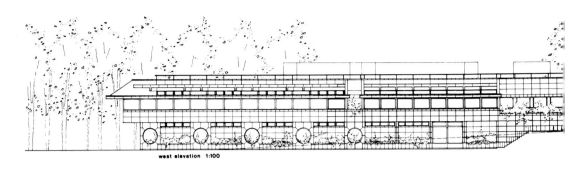

west elevation 1:100

The promoters envisage a linear university plan with a pedestrian precinct and/or a formal approach avenue as a central space. The future sequence of teaching facilities to the north of the future central space may then be consistently serviced from Lower Woods Road via a series of screened car parks. The continuous zone of trees between the teaching buildings and the car park also provides a secondary east-west pedestrian route culminating in the proposed wooded area north of the library which in turn screens the car parks from the western approach.

The library seems to be in a strategic position to allow a possible future adjacent building – the College Hall, the Circulation Concourse. The proposed Concourse will thus act as an entrance or 'gateway' to the main pedestrian precinct.

This grouping of facilities common to the entire college – the student areas, the hall, the cafeteria and the library – is likely to become the hub of the college. The proposed Concourse will remain the main entrance to the college but may be linked in future with a sequence of minor entrances from the north into the pedestrian precinct.

The approach to the main entrance may relate either to the north-south proposed avenue of trees linking the residential accommodation with the pedestrian precinct, or to the proposed Concourse.

For day to day use the library is mainly designed on a single level to be entered from the pedestrian precinct, with a lower level, which contains the text book library, also approachable from the service-parking zone.

The library is planned around a central top-lit reading room with the private and semi-private reading cubicles arranged around it. The central small reading room is formed and contained by the three main building elements or zones, each of which may subsequently be modified and further developed in accordance with detailed observations and requirements.

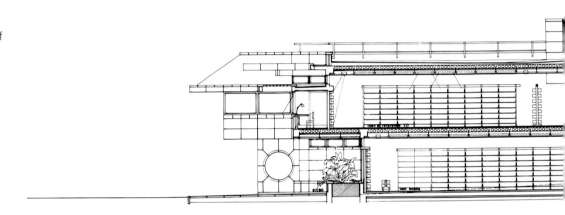

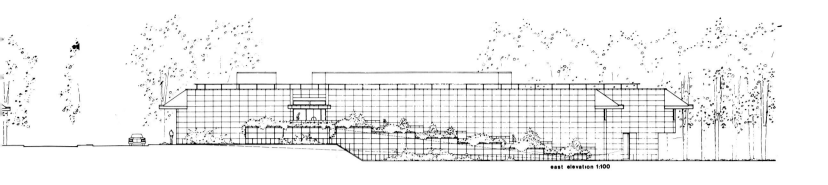

east elevation 1:100

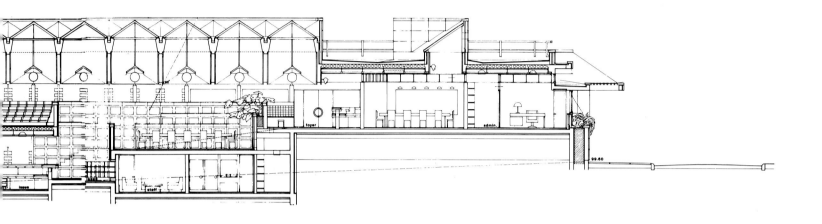

foyer   admin.

issue   staff   99.60

1984

TOMORROW'S THINK TANK TODAY

Central to a new order of student prizes the RIBA will put on offer in 1985 is the idea of an annual international competition set up around an architect of distinction.

Tomorrow's Think Tank Today, sponsored for the 1984 Festival of Architecture by the RIBA and Sinclair Research Ltd, was devised and assessed by Sir Norman Foster with Sir Clive Sinclair and Professor Edmund Happold as co-jurors – architect, client and engineer.

The competition drew in 284 entries. Of these 154 were from 29 British schools and 130 were from 30 schools in 15 countries overseas, which must be a record.

It was encouraging to see such a large response – nearly 300 entries from such diverse locations as Japan, America, Canada, South Africa and Australia as well as continental Europe and the United Kingdom. It would seem that the decision not to pick a specific site was helpful because it enabled people to design within their own national cultures.

As the architect on the jury I felt a special responsibility with Ted Happold not only to exercise value judgements on the merits of competing schemes, but also to enable Sir Clive to take initiatives in his dual role as assessor and potential client. It is therefore appropriate to quote his responses to the various schemes. The most satisfying aspect of the selection process was the unanimity among the three assessors, which was total and without qualifications. This was both surprising and reassuring in view of the extreme diversity of entries. *Sir Norman Foster*

1st Prize: *Andrew Birds (bottom), Polytechnic of Central London, UK*

2nd Prize: *Robert Mullan, University of Bath, UK*

Joint 3rd Prizes: *David Naessens (top), University College, Dublin, Eire; David Turnbull, University of Bath, UK; Anya van der Merwe and Mathew Maszewski, University of Cape Town, South Africa*

Judges: *Sir Norman Foster, Sir Clive Sinclair, Professor Edmund Happold (opposite)*

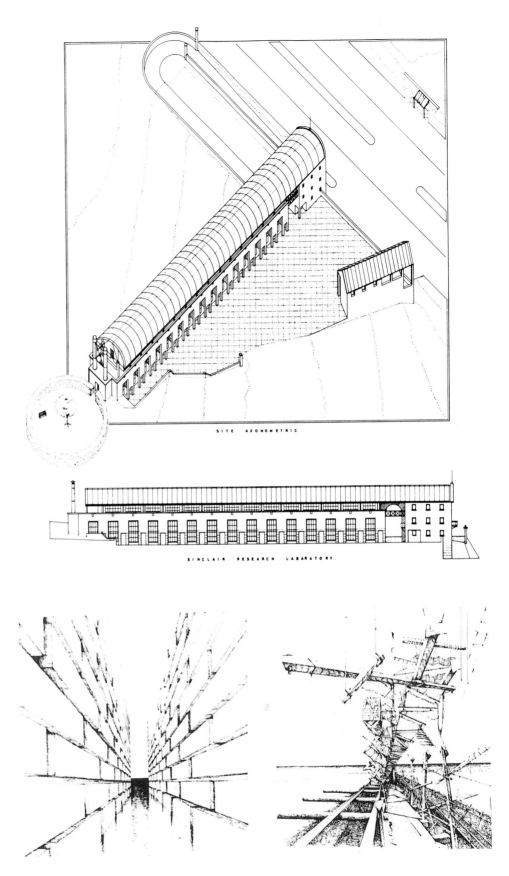

SITE AXONOMETRIC

SINCLAIR RESEARCH LABORATORY

1st PRIZE
ANDREW BIRDS
Polytechnic of Central
London, UK

In this scheme two man-made cliffs of laboratories are inserted into the rock of a coastline separated by a vertical void containing circulation. The laboratories are modules which appear as gargantuan building blocks articulated by glass strips. As a project it could be read at several levels – a poetic allegory for instance with its overtones of medieval alchemy and a central space of such disordered menace that its driftwood imagery recalled Hieronymus Bosch or even John Wyndham's Triffids. But aside from such themes as order versus disorder, the overall vision produced a compelling image which captured the imagination of the jurors, each with their own interpretations.

I think it stands out head and shoulders. It is so original, it is immediately exciting and then when you look into it you think, well is that really going to work? And then you get beyond that and see that it can work. It's a very courageous design, I think . . .

Obviously in a competition we are looking for original talent. There is nothing in the competition which I think is remotely as original as this. It is startlingly original, and yet it is all too easy to be original without being plausible. But this is plausible. It is right on the edge. You've got to stretch a bit to believe it can be done, but I do believe it could be. If you got the site and were allowed to build such a building, I think it would be marvellous. Just the sort of thing I would like to see.

I might have to argue with the architect a bit over a detail or two. I might say, is there enough outside light coming in, or something of that sort, and of course a lot of the details have yet to be filled in on it. But yes, I can imagine loving to work in a building like that. *Sir Clive Sinclair*

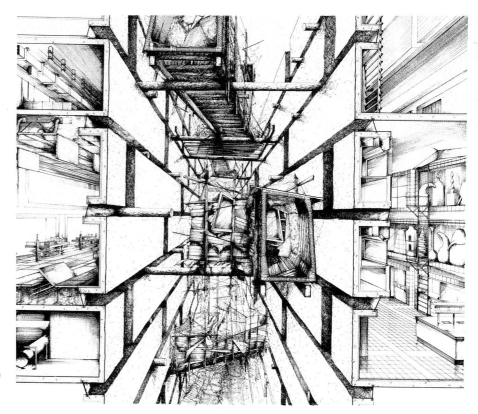

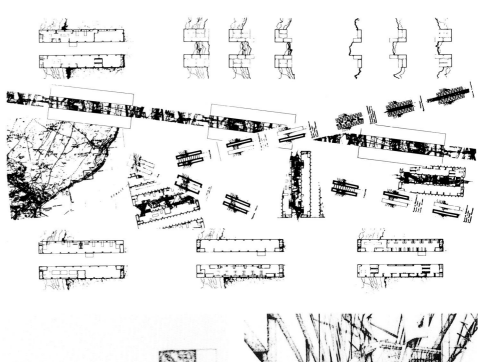

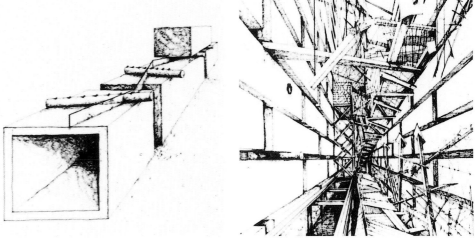

2nd PRIZE

ROBERT MULLAN
University of Bath, UK
A Walk in the Woods

Evocatively titled, sensitively conceived and presented with a high degree of professionalism, this scheme was as down-to-earth as the previous one was enigmatic and conjectural. The 'walk in the woods' was an interweave of landscaping, cor-ten steel, brick and glass. Its planning was deceptively simple, informal and relaxed with overtones of Mies van der Rohe – a route which meanders through the trees and around clusters of buildings. Although some of its details were unresolved it was simple, economic and buildable.

Again it looks lovely because the prospects would be wonderful from any window. I believe that you would get excellent work from people in that sort of site. He kept the building plain and simple in tune with the woods and lawns around – there would also be much opportunity for people to meet by chance. *Sir Clive Sinclair*

A WALK IN THE WOODS

SITE AS EXISTING
TO DODINGTON HOUSE
GRASSED RIDE
BRISTOL CHANNEL
M4
EXISTING ESTATE GATES
LODGE

SITE PROPOSALS
CAR PARK   SERVICE YARD
RECEPTION
VIEWS
GATES RETAINED

MATERIALS
COR-TEN STEEL IN STANDARD
I SECTIONS
POLISHED PLATE GLASS
DARK BROWN AND BUFF FACING BRICKS
NEW ROAD SURFACES OF
REINFORCED GRASS
INTERIOR CARPETED
THROUGHOUT EXCEPT 'DIRTY' AREAS

Sinclair

M4

LOCATION PLAN 1:2500

GROUND FLOOR PLAN 1:200

SINCLAIR RESEARCH
DODINGTON PARK

19

RECENT WORK

BIRDS PORTCHMOUTH RUSSUM
Avenue de Chartres Car Park

The Stirling-trained partners Birds Portchmouth Russum formed a practice after winning the Chichester competition with the largest urban creation in the UK to date, the Avenue de Chartres car park. Previous projects submitted to other public sector competitions include a new town for Bologna, in which car parking played a significant role.

At a pragmatic level the Chichester scheme is very successful. Among other things it uses distributor roads to prevent blocking the route to and from the exit, and colour-coded pedestrian aisles to give access to the walkway at first-floor level. The project makes a major intervention into urban design by screening the historic city from its transport infrastructure.

Located at the main entrance to the city between the medieval cathedral and city wall, the project is integrated with its surroundings since the section of the walkway on the north face (brick parapet on one side, shrubs on the other) is derived from the medieval walls, while the towers echo the verticality and bold scale of the cathedral. This historicism is set off against the concrete and steel mesh of the car-parking structure.

The world of value (the historic city) and the world of utility (the goods yard) are counterpoised rather than amalgamated in the Chichester project, defining it as not so much a retreat from the heroic ambitions of Modernism as a welcome acceptance of the difference between the aesthetic and the everyday.

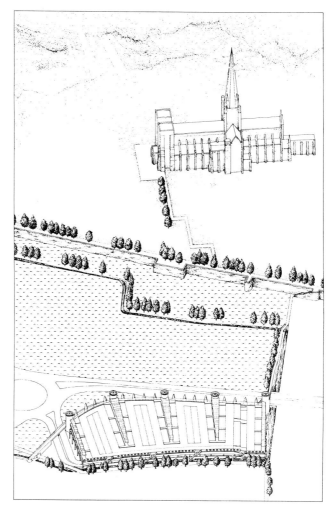

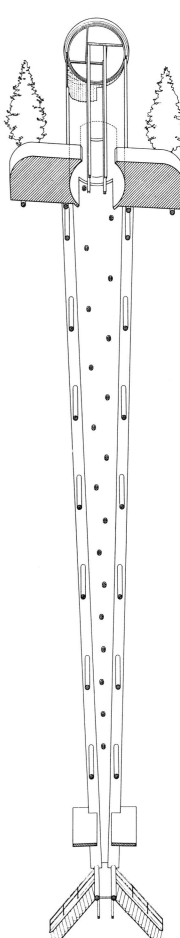

JUDGE
EDMUND HAPPOLD
Commerzbank, Frankfurt, Germany

During recent moves to upgrade the financial area of Frankfurt, the Commerzbank held a competition between a great many architects for a 'green' tower block to be built within a complex of existing buildings on a central site. The architect, Christoph Ingenhoven, selected Frei Otto as consultant and Buro Happold as engineers.

The entry was for a circular tower 44 storeys high with a diameter of 42 metres and with a height to aspect ratio of 10:5. The concept allows for a central core with lifts and internal stairs and lenticular gardens at the four sides of the building. This leaves a cross-shaped plan for the internal building, which guarantees that all offices are less than seven metres away from daylight and the natural ventilation provided by the internal gardens.

The 'radical' starting point in the Frankfurt project was to strive to produce a naturally ventilated building depending on the stack effect for an element of forced ventilation. Wind forces at the top of a 44-storey building are significant. The solution was to put a shield around the building diverting the energy of the wind forces yet allowing the outside fresh air to leak through into the buffer zone between the barrier and the building.

Such a 'shroud' around the building presented the potential of a skin into which was incorporated minimalist tie bracing against the high lateral winds on the tall building. It is proposed that the system of louvres in both inner and outer skins would be controlled to allow night-time cooling of the occupied space, thereby reducing the building's potential cooling demand. In winter the enclosed gardens will act as solaria, collecting heat from the winter sun. This heat can be trapped and moved around the building to the cooler, north-facing zones and here the interaction of structure and environmental design is once again important.

The relationship of the tower to the city is important and it encourages users and staff of the bank to adopt the environmentally friendly course of travelling to work by public transport – surely one of the main aims of a green building.

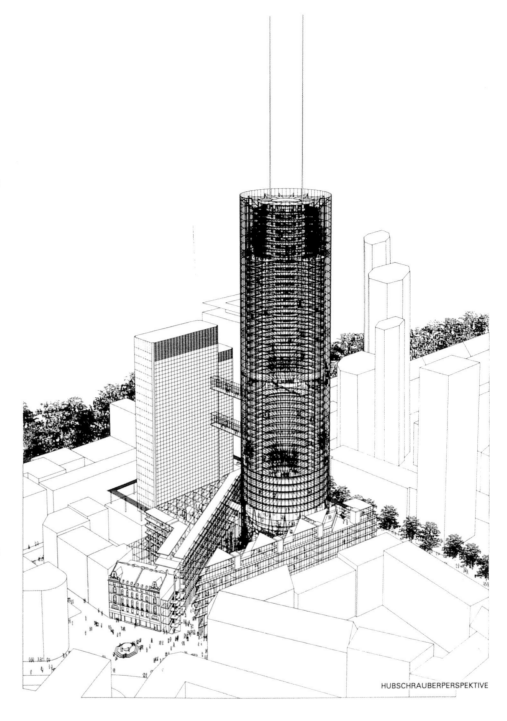

HUBSCHRAUBERPERSPEKTIVE

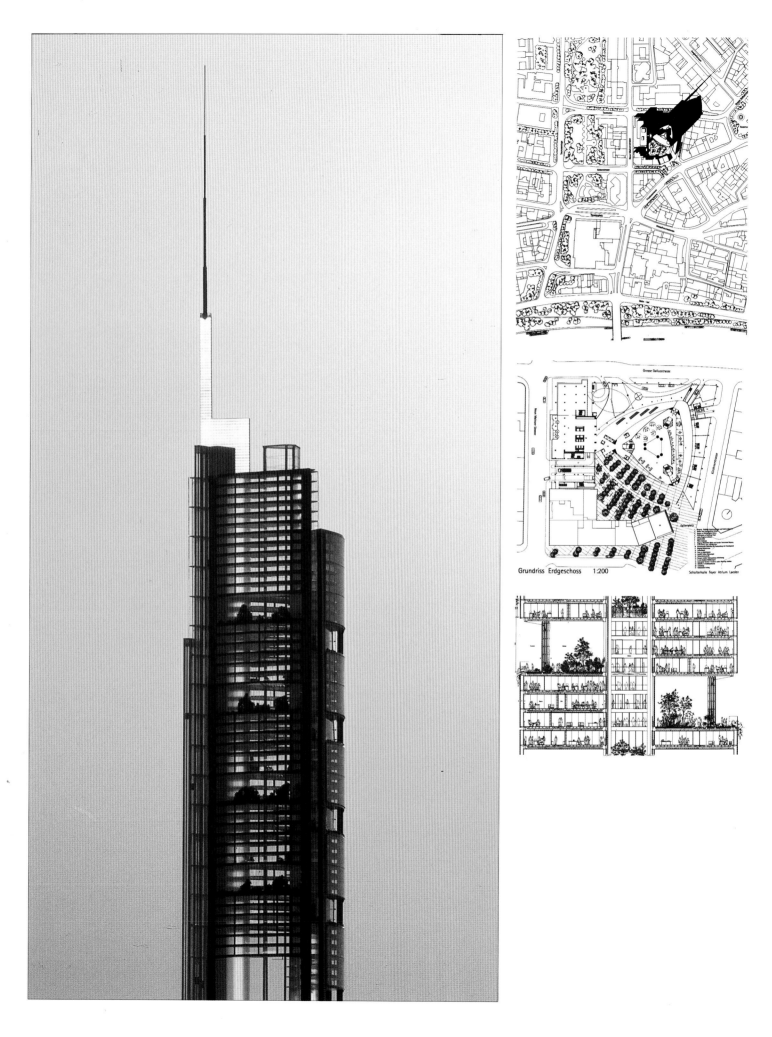

Grundriss Erdgeschoss 1:200

JUDGE
FOSTER ASSOCIATES
Commerzbank, Frankfurt, Germany

Foster Associates' success in the competition for a new headquarters for Commerzbank, situated at the centre of Frankfurt, represents a decisive step in the practice's move towards increasingly sophisticated buildings.

The bank, like other major German businesses, embraces 'green' policies. It currently occupies a number of buildings spread around Frankfurt, with its principal offices in a 1970s tower behind Kaiserplatz. The new building will adjoin the latter, with provision made in the Foster scheme for its possible eventual replacement.

Norman Foster has always regretted that the 'garden in the sky' planned for the Hongkong Bank failed to materialise – 'the most significant loss in that building', he says. At Frankfurt, he has been able to return to the theme and to adopt a system of natural air-conditioning which would have been inconceivable in Hong Kong.

The form of the block is triangular – three 'petals' spreading out from a central stem. The petals are the office floors, the stem a great central slot running right up the tower and providing cooling draughts to all floors. At every third floor, the offices are interspersed with gardens staggered around the height of the tower, so that every office has a view into a garden and great expanses of unbroken office space are avoided. In a tower of this height, conventional opening windows are impractical but windows have been designed to open behind a windbreak layer of glazing.

At ground level, the building sits amidst a huddle of 19th-century blocks. A new courtyard is to be created, glazed over and opened to the public, with gardens and restaurants, as an alternative to the usual tower-in-piazza formula. The tower does not try to lord it over its surroundings, but rather strives to respect them and to address the city streets.

The detailed designs for Commerzbank will concentrate on heightening the sense of identity and place in the building, which is set to become the first of the really big green office buildings constructed in the late 20th century.

1985

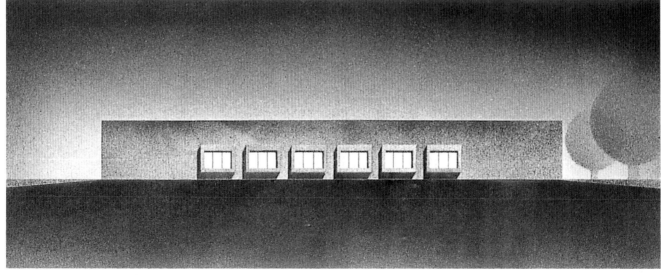

CONCORD GALLERY

A 'representational' design is likely to be visually related to tradition, vernacular, history and recognition of the familiar. A building which is 'abstract' is likely to be influenced by the 20th-century language of design, developed from Cubism, Constructivism, de Stijl, Futurism etc. Both characteristics could co-exist as they do in the other arts, as they do separately in the work of David Hockney and Anthony Caro.

Can we extend the contemporary vocabulary of architecture by combining, conjoining, collaging and juxtaposing these and other aspects? Or should the distinction between tradition and abstraction be maintained, clearly expressed, separated, counterbalanced, articulated?

The architect was asked to design an appropriate new gallery to house the representational and abstract works of Hockney and Caro.

A wealthy collector decided to bequeath his large collection of Hockneys and Caros to the public. The purpose of the benefaction is to bring painting, sculpture and architecture into a positive relationship for the public benefit. The new gallery was to be built in a small municipal park, close to a town centre. The site was level and on grass without features, and orientation could be in any direction.

It was necessary to create an interior setting equally appropriate to Hockney's paintings (there are no works on paper) and Caro's sculptures. Whether these spaces should be rooms or open space, and combined and/or separated, could be the basis of an architectural solution. The Caros should be housed indoors though a few pieces could be located outside but not 'au naturel'– he would prefer his outside sculptures to be terraced and semi-contained in dwarf wall settings. Internal spaces for both artists should have daylight, though direct sunlight should not fall on the paintings. The sculptures should be in spaces at least four metres high.

In addition to an entrance hall, with information facilities and adjoining toilets, cloakrooms etc, there should be a lounge/reading room. Also, there should be a changing exhibition space of approximately 300 square metres (not related to the permanent collections) for temporary exhibitions; this area should not be daylit. Mechanical plant space will be necessary. Six small offices and a staffroom for six technical staff is needed with adjoining cloakrooms and toilet facilities.

1st Prize: *Kay Ngee Tan, Architectural Association, UK*
2nd Prize: *Felim Dunne (top), University College, Dublin, Eire*
3rd Prize: *Farahbod Nakhaei, University of Strathclyde, UK*
Commended: *Hans-Jürgen Tarrey (opposite), Technische University Braunschweig, Germany; Farahbod Nakhaei (bottom), University of Strathclyde, UK*
Judges: *Sir James Stirling, Lord McAlpine, Alan Bowness, Janet Turner*

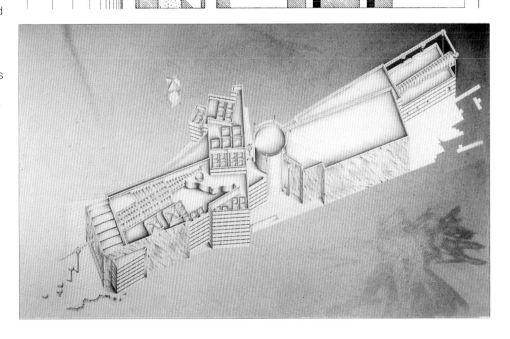

1st PRIZE

KAY NGEE TAN
Architectural Association, UK

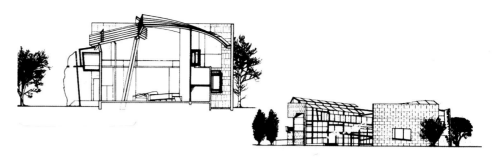

There is something very special about the first prize winner, Kay Ngee Tan of the Architectural Association in London. A student from Singapore who has spent his last three or four years in London, he is a very sophisticated person, and immediately when you start looking at this project you realise that it is not one of those buildings that can be simply explained away. It is the product of a very well informed mind making a comment back to the artist in terms of his architecture; he even quotes the title of one of Hockney's drawings, *We Two Together Clinging*. He makes the building a response – in walls, in passages, in staircases – to the two boys clinging together in the Hockney drawing. I think that it is a very strange building, it is a very delicate building, and it is a very self-assured building. It is one of those things that older architects and teachers are always looking for, student work that suddenly makes you sit up hard and say, 'My God, these guys have already moved into a new territory, and that makes you feel that all the things that you do are relatively sterile, crude and slow.' *Peter Cook*

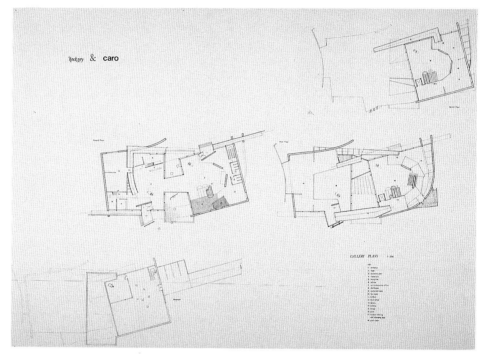

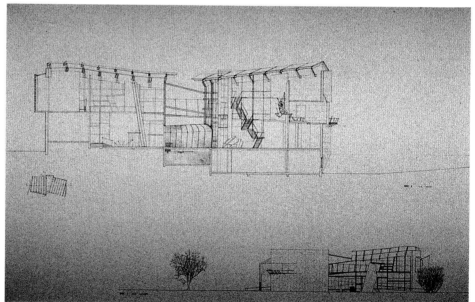

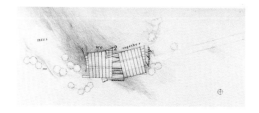

2nd PRIZE

FELIM DUNNE
University College Dublin, Eire

Students from Dublin have featured quite heavily in this competition, and there is certainly a powerful architectural position at the University College there, a Rationalist-inspired position with obvious close linkages to Italy and to Germany. Felim Dunne is the second-prize winner and his is a beautifully drawn project, a very good example of its kind. It is not only accurately drawn, but it's drawn with a tremendous control over the pieces of information on the paper. I think it is the characteristic of all the main prize winners that they leave you in no doubt as to their sense of priorities. If they bother to draw a line then they are using drawings to make the most rhetorical points. Mr Dunne is no exception to this; when he uses a coved moulding or when he uses some cross hatching he is using it very powerfully to as it were expunge every other kind of architectural thought away, to attack it. On one of the drawings, he shows a scroll as if the piece of paper were being unwound, and he is making a statement about the purpose of drawings as a whole when he does that.

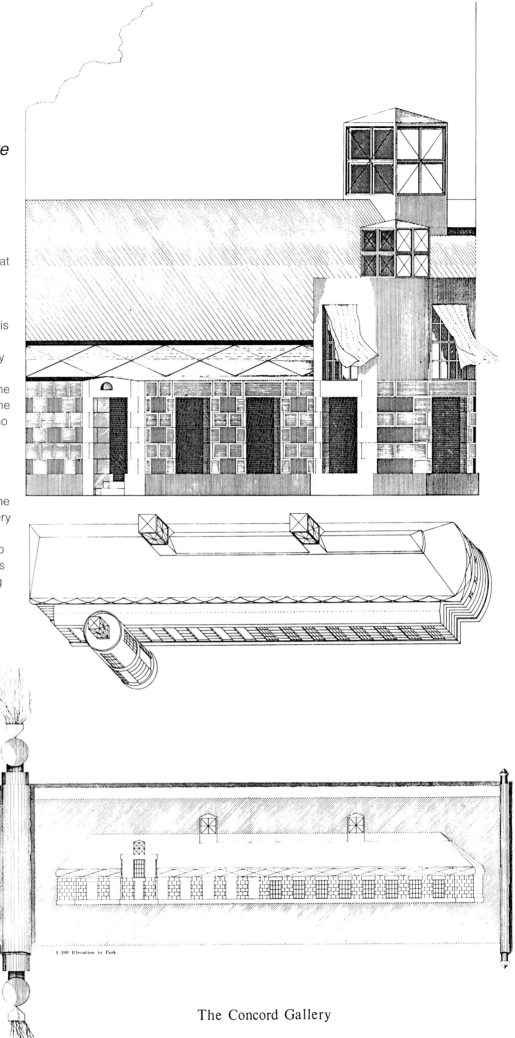

The Concord Gallery

RECENT WORK

KAY NGEE TAN
How to love a man who
doesn't love me

Eight screens of differing size, arranged at intervals, capture along them seven long, linear gaps. The clearly defined space in front of the plains contrasts with the veiled moments seen behind only fleetingly.

The white painted screens reveal their hidden details only after close inspection. Dashes of muddy brown and blue at different corners are like blemishes or violent actions that have been white-washed over. Doors open at high and low levels, figures emerge. The placement of steps on the stage is symbolic and pro-vokes various interpretations – like hopes we look up to and long for, like many other moments of subtle meanings in this sophis-ticatedly choreographed piece of work.

FELIM DUNNE
Dublin Warehouse Conversion

A contribution to the urban regeneration of Dublin was the conversion of a former banana-ripening warehouse on Liffey Quays for the Irish rock group U2 by Felim Dunne. The original structure was a pair of sheds set side by side with interiors rising clear to trussed roofs behind a double red-brick, two-storey facade. This single-volume space has been split to provide two floors, the upper becoming the business headquarters for U2. The brief demanded a series of spaces of different sizes, a large office, smaller private offices, conference room and service areas including a gym. The solid timber trusses of the roof define the space beneath them, dividing the volume into a series of bays. Furniture and finishes were kept simple and discreet so as not to distract from the original structure and fabric.

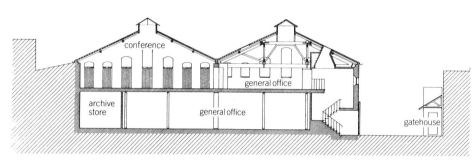

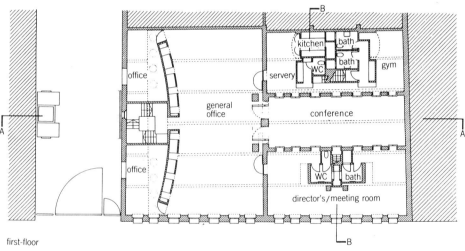

first-floor

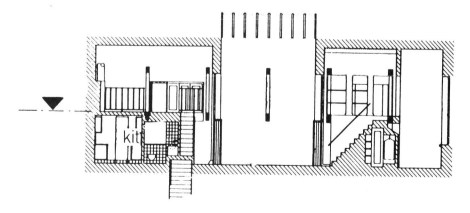

JUDGE

*JAMES STIRLING AND
MICHAEL WILFORD IN
ASSOCIATION WITH
MITSUBISHI ESTATES
Kyoto Centre, 1991*

We view the site as a threshold between the traditional city to the north, enclosed by hills to the east and west, and the future Technological City to be built in the south. We propose symbolic and functional gateways leading to public crossings over the barrier of the railway tracks which presently divides the city centre into two halves.

The Oval Plaza is a semi-contained space connecting with a new Citizens' Bridge (lined with shops) which spans the tracks connecting the north and south sides of the city. A feature of the design is the two north-south crossings over the railway tracks. The Citizens' Bridge spanning from the Oval Plaza to the Shinkansen Station shopping area is the primary 'free pathway'. Retail facilities are distributed along the site to maximise shopping including cafe/restaurants and speciality stores around the hotel and under the Cultural Centre.

The size of the Cultural Centre is greater than required in the competition. The volume containing the image facilities is planned as a winter garden with a large floor area for exhibitions and public events.

Four levels of basement are vertically divided into two zones including a double-height shopping 'street' providing linear connection between the existing subway station and the JR Station Concourse. This acts as a spine for a new underground shopping centre with connections to existing basement shopping areas. A high-speed people mover suspended in the 'street' provides quick access for subway and station passengers travelling the length of the development. These proposals respond to urbanistic concerns and tidal people movements with morning and evening peaks of activity.

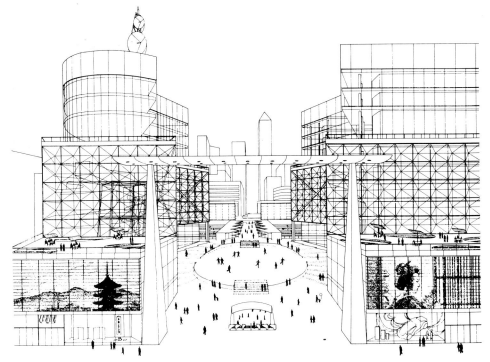

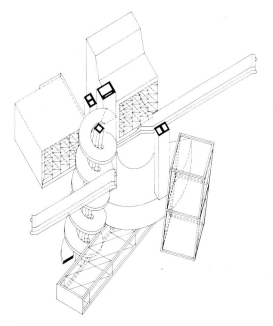

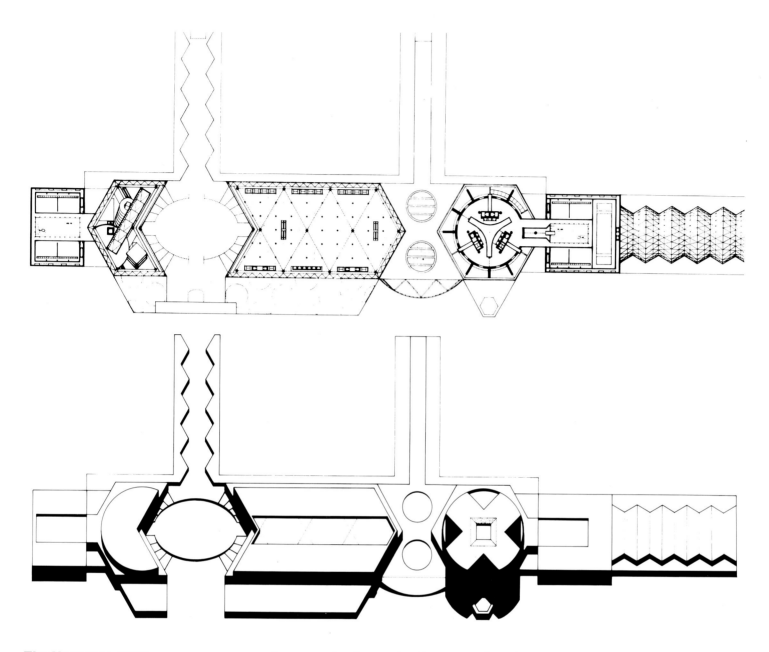

The Year was 1985

Studio 402 at PLC had been cleared, dozens of large cardboard boxes packed with A1 sheets filled the space. A formidable heavy wooden crate from Moscow was prised open, lighter packaging from Peking fell off, entries from Eastern Europe were released from their collective wrapping. How would Communists house Caro and Hockney works? Had Western fine art obsessions really penetrated the ideological curtain? Was the language of architecture in schools from over 40 countries up to the challenge? There was keen anticipation over the response to an inventive programme inviting spatial and cultural dialectic. A comfortable (large) chair, continuous sustenance and six able-bodied students to parade the schemes was the formula devised to attempt the impossible. His name had drawn 950 entries, a record still. I knew he was quick.

As an examiner in my school he extracted the essence of projects in seconds, his judgement impeccable and generous with a bias towards risk, naturally. But this was ridiculous! There were 950 in one day: the thumb pointed up (in), down (out) or horizontal (hold). By six o'clock 35 were shortlisted. 'Allen, just go through these and make sure they have answered the brief. See you for lunch tomorrow.' 'Hey, hold it! I can't do that, one of my students may be in this lot.' 'See you tomorrow.' After lunch with his other jurors, Alistair McAlpine, Alan Bowness and Janet Turner, he dissected each scheme without spilling a drop of blood, let the conversation flow and knowingly deflected those prejudices which did not coincide with his own. The dialogue was rich and when his choice was picked everyone realised it was theirs too. Typically he christened the architecture of the winner 'slippy-slidey'. I wondered,

foolishly, whether he had let any good ones go through, but a subsequent riffle through the reject boxes confirmed a flawless judgement. James Stirling, the greatest British architect of this century, we salute you and mourn your absence from a celebration of young architecture, your endorsement of which legitimised the whole enterprise. Allen Cunningham, July 1992

1986

A LAST RESORT

Joint 1st Prize: *Jonathan Wilson (opposite), University of Bath, UK; Stewart Brown, University of Cape Town, South Africa; Kati Miettinen, Helsinki University of Technology, Finland*
Commended: *Susan Watson (bottom), University of Toronto, Canada; Helen Landers (top), Humberside College of Higher Education, UK*
Judges: *Aldo van Eyck, Dick Hillenius, Hannie van Eyck, Julyan Wickham, Rick Mather, and Lucien Lafour*

The competition was for a last resort for marsupials and monotremes in which these exotic creatures might live, be observed and studied – and even escape possible extinction. This unconventional subject was selected in the hope of subverting fashionable style-mongering. It soon became clear that almost everybody had chosen to play the game properly, some exceedingly well, others less well and others again – a few – rather foolishly. Too many diverted their design attention to rather fortuitous and extraneous issues – sometimes coupled with moralistic gestures which animal-captivity is bound to draw forth. There were those which avoided 'architecture' altogether out of principle, or rejected building anything at all new where visible. Instead great caves, ancient catacombs, obsolete U-bahn tunnels and a mammoth oil tanker are recycled for our pouched guests.

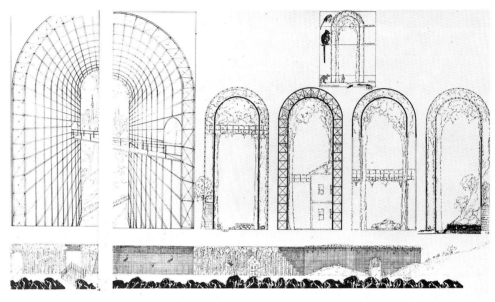

The shift away from current trends that colour everything alike worldwide did bring out differences between schools and countries. From France, just geometrics in concrete, with attention to what is inanimate only; from England nothing at all of that kind, as the results show; from Japan nothing that belongs to this world; from China nothing that is not a bit plain and didactic. What I call hut and humble proposals arrived from many places. Although these needn't have looked so African, they were far more acceptable than the 'city halls for marsupials' kind, of which there were luckily only a few. There were animal parks out in the open providing for a wide range of species. Some dealt in detail with the requirements of individual species, whereas others stuck to general ideas; but high quality schemes were to be found either way.

Generally speaking more sense of reality, and less indifference as to what a building is required to fulfil, would have been welcome. But then the tendency to 'escape' is today universal among architects.

Taking the perplexities of the brief into account, the number of entries with commendable features is considerable – many more than the three winners and 15 mentions certainly. *Aldo van Eyck*

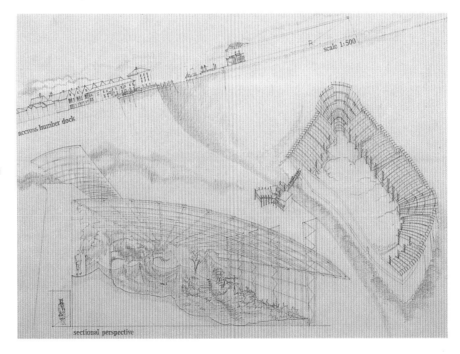

sectional perspective

JOINT 1st PRIZE

JONATHAN WILSON
University of Bath, UK

An admirably accomplished piece of work and unanimously appreciated. The way the climatic conditions are made lovingly adjustable is as ingenious as it is endearing – endearingly ingenious. The 'architecture' is quiet, efficient and pleasantly effective – all three diminishing properties. The way people can creep up close to the animals unnoticed, observing them from various angles and levels, is superlative. Then there is the good servicing throughout the inside; and the siting in the wood with its walk round the pretty clearings for kangaroos. Whether those indoor trees would grow as imagined is questionable. Art and science coincide nicely here; and that is probably how it should be in architecture, strange profession, though it would become less intractable – and easier too – if that could only be taken for granted.

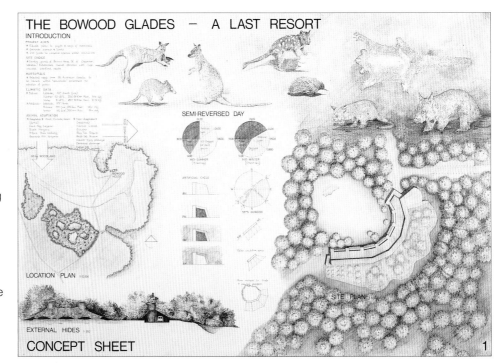

THE BOWOOD GLADES — A LAST RESORT

CONCEPT SHEET

FLOOR PLANS & GLADE VIEW 1500, NTS

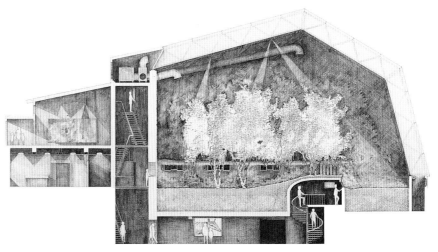

JOINT 1st PRIZE

STEWART BROWN
*University of Cape Town,
South Africa*

Of all the larger environmental park-like proposals, this one is certainly the most convincing gesture, although not as fully resolved as the other two winners which are, of course, quite different in kind, size and climatic resonance.

The real gist is the spectacular site and the grip the scheme has on it. With the sea-horizon on one side and the huge animal enclosure on the other as you walk along on that great wall between the two, people will witness what they'll want to witness again. The places where the interior slips underneath and beyond the wall so as to become 'exterior' space are really good; also the way the outdoor spaces for the various species from the largest to the smallest fit together within the overall perimeter. As for the different buildings – public facilities, animal clinic, guest house etc – these are all quite plausible, and fitted into the landscape carefully, though the entrance is rather more impressive than is good for it!

So far so good. What worries me, I'm afraid, are the walls separating the various species from each other: their exorbitant height and nervous irregularity, with arbours extending still further upwards, result in dark jungle-like depths between the walls which would not be congenial to animals attuned to Australia's outback. Then there is the cage-like zigzagging walkway with its intended moralistic message: people inside, animals outside – which is a pity.

The enormous roof over most of the smaller outdoor spaces is drawn without any structure at all, so that no idea can be formed as to how it would affect the animal world below – and it will, huge as it is. But all the queries aside (they can be resolved), the main gesture remains outstanding.

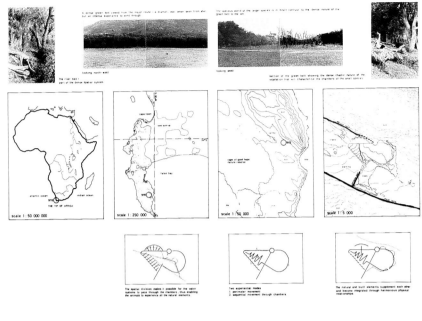

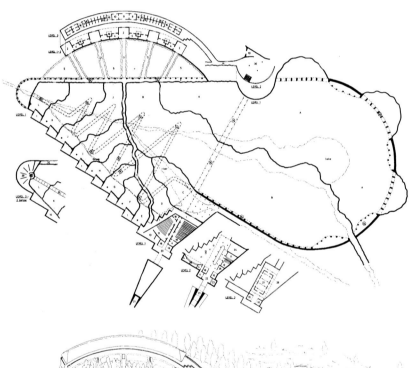

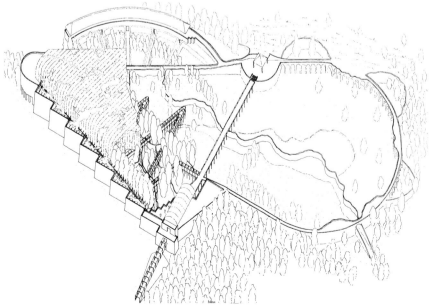

JOINT 1st PRIZE

KATI MIETTINEN
Helsinki University
of Technology, Finland

A real architect's proposal if ever there was one, judged favourably by architects and confirmed zoologically. That's as it should be; no trivia – nothing necessary evaded. Done well, with competence, insight, sensitivity and ingenuity. The only dream which may perhaps not come true is the one about full-size trees growing indoors! Never mind, this proposal shows that buildings can be pleasant places without that much help from nature – so it wouldn't matter if the trees failed to live up to expectations. As for the animals inside 'buildings', we've got used to cats and dogs in living rooms, horses in stables (if we no longer miss the sound, sight and smell of them in our streets that is only because it is too long ago) birds in cages, imperial lions in front of banks – even sacred cows amid modern traffic in India.

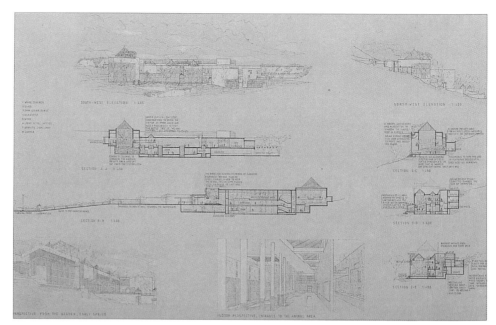

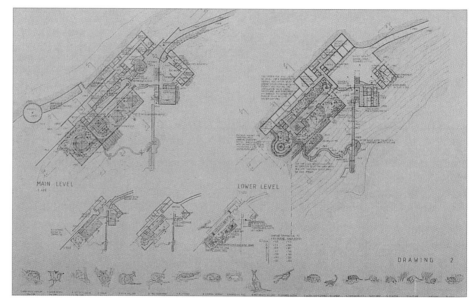

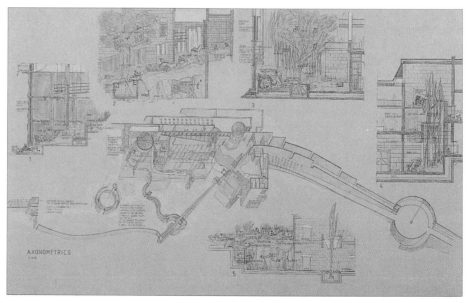

RECENT WORK

KATI MIETTINEN
House by Brisbane River

This is for a peaceful suburban site by Brisbane River with an easement on the northern side, east-west orientation (east to river) and a wonderful view along the river bend to Old Walter Talor Bridge. The house is pushed close to the waterfront, and main living areas are arranged cross the site on fill. Garage, music room, laundry, staircase, bathrooms and dressing room form a spine on the southern boundary to close off the neighbouring house.

The client is a Dutch family of five. The brief was for a four-bedroom house with a rustic, Mediterranean, cosy feeling for outdoor-indoor living and relaxed entertaining. A European, contemporary feeling was to be expressed with 'streamlined', clear massing and detailing.

The resolution was to create a semi-open, flowing space for entry, dining and living, connecting to the kitchen and opening to the river terrace as well as to the pool patio and cane-covered entry walkway. With the use of dropped ceilings, built-in TV cabinet and fireplace, curved stuccoed wall with display openings, semi-open kitchen partition and a suspended painting display board in the conservatory, the space has been given differing experiences of form, light, scale, intimacy and visual interest. Climatic aspects, orientation and light, wind, cross-ventilation, rain and views from and within the house were under consideration. The main bedroom has a bay window giving an extra feeling of space. The dressing room is open to the river and garden. Upstairs bedrooms and study with a balcony are reached via a light and breezy staircase of stained plywood leading to a hall dominated by a void, connecting to an entry hall and curved blue wall reflecting the downstairs stucco wall and concealing the yellow and white bathroom. The upstairs windows are shaded with adjustable timber shutters.

All materials are natural, easily maintained and with a warm, relaxed feeling. Rough render, terracotta, stained timbers, cane ceilings and handrails, coir and limewash contrast with the delicate artwork and tie in with the antique Dutch timber furniture and client's interesting lifestyle.

FABERY DE JONGE RESIDENCE
TWIGG STREET INDOOROPILLY
1989-90
KATI

JONATHAN WILSON
Housing for the Elderly

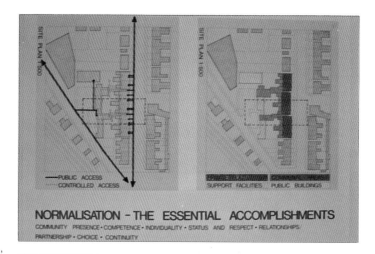

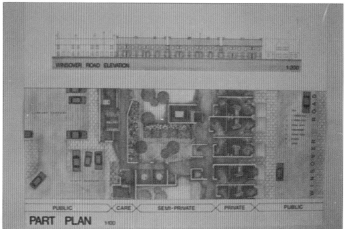

Elderly people would be best cared for within their own converted homes, though economic reasons may prevent this. Yet creating a familiar environment may provide community presence, freedom, dignity, respect and continuity. The proposal here is for individual terraced 'homes', reinforcing the existing domestic scale of the area. The terraces house ground- and first-floor flats. Each flat faces both the street and the shared conservatory and gardens. The inclusion of public facilities is important to ensure that the site becomes part of the community.

The population likely to become resident in this accommodation is today living locally in what may have been the family home for many years. If this is the most suitable form of accommodation for the frail elderly, then the building type for their housing in the year 2000 already exists.

STEWART BROWN
Entrance Building to Underground Caves, Kluterthöhle, Ennepetal, Germany

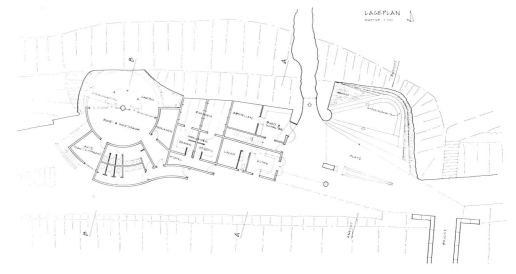

This facility needed to house a ticket office, store and social room with toilet and shower; a kiosk with toilet and store as well as a flat for the owner; toilets, dressing and shower rooms for the public; a sanitary/doctor's room and a rest/waiting area for asthma patients who visit the caves.

The building form is the result of two primary concerns, the movement of people and the specific topographical site factors.

Because of the sensitive nature of the protected site, natural materials were used. The construction is timber as well as the external cladding, while the base of the building is stone, which links with the cave entrance. For ecological reasons the sloping roof has been grassed.

JUDGE

ALDO VAN EYCK
The Wheels of Heaven . . .

The church today, I feel, is notoriously impervious to poetry. Can one possibly cope with this negative, I ask myself: only if one can provide scope for what is thus missing, is my answer.

Listening to everything this chapel is to fulfil and avoid, I noticed a deep-rooted vagueness – even doubt – on the part of the client, the protestant 'Church and World' movement, as to the ultimate relevance of a church as a particular place.

I mention this because I found the lead I needed in this gratifying sense of uncertainty. If I could only translate this doubt into built form – scope for ambivalent meaning – hence for poetry also – would perhaps ensue.

I was thinking about such twin-phenomena as inside-outside; open-closed; many few; alone-together; individual-collective, when the following twin-image came to my mind. It helped.

People seated concentrically in a hollow, gazing inwards towards the centre; and people seated concentrically on a hill, gazing outwards towards the horizon.

Two kinds of centrality? Two ways of being together – or alone?

The images are ambivalent – though the hill reveals what the hollow may conceal: that man is both centre-bound and horizon-bound. Both hill and hollow, horizon and centre, are shared by all seated concentrically either way; both link and both lure (the horizon and the shifting centre, the centre and the shifting horizon).

To be thoughtful in a space, moreover, one's thoughts must be able to wander – one even needs to be without them – certainly in a church!

The attention of *all* should not be summoned peremptorily by a single central place and what occurs there. Instead the attention of *each* should be granted liberally to a number of places.

From the very start, I wanted the church to be multi-centred, but not a-central! I wanted a single space clearly articulated (the singular embracing the plural; the plural contained in the singular).

The centres or articulated places which resulted are not the same, though they have equal validity. In fact there is no fixed place-hierarchy – the quadripartite articulation (three plus one) takes care of that. Whilst

the different 'centres' are precisely determined, their use is not. I hope they are also multi-suggestive – possess the right scope – for this is what multi-centrality can effect (through articulation but not through the lack of it).

Between tall trees cylindrical concrete columns – between these, screenlike walls and, low over column and wall, a framework of concrete beams spanning horizontally and carrying four circular skylight structures, the configuration of which, seen from below, I named 'The Wheels of Heaven'.

The chapel opens upwards suddenly in different directions taking in the treetops, but also downwards here and there towards the soil. In between it tends inwards – churchwards – and is translucent rather than transparent.

The four circles together have two points of focus. They are situated in the 'path' which passes through the entire building from door to door and beyond through the courts into the park. One 'encounters' two essentially ambivalent places: one for the sacrament of the Lord's Supper? The other for the spoken word?

As to the complex diagonality, I think it assists the idea of multi-centrality. The seating arrangement (only a suggestion)

exploits the various implicit directions so that each person may experience the same space in a different way according to which group he chooses – proximity, too, according to individual inclination. Where the diagonals cross there is, for once, just space!

One of the circles is amphitheatrical; it can be used for small gatherings during weekdays, baptisms, marriages or choir. The other three circumscribe mildly without asserting their centres. (All three groups are shown facing the pulpit here.)

The spaces between the framework of beams and the skylight structures are, I believe, quite enigmatic. They are intermediary, an in-between world which holds and transmits that which is outside and above the roof to those inside; sky, passing clouds, trees, birds – from season to season – and light which passes through the 'wheels' into the space below and falls on the people, as it should.

It is no longer my intention to stress the quadripartite articulation in the floor by means of different materials, but the curved railings will remain.

The chapel is only 12 feet high. It may, if I am lucky, acquire something of the altitude of light itself. I leave that to the wheels.

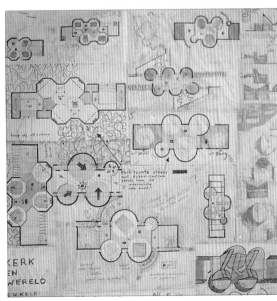

1987

NEW IN THE OLD

Much of the interest in the RIBA International Student Competitions has been the display of national characteristics in the works submitted. In 1985 the subject itself was local and precise. Consequently each entry was at the centre of a complex amalgam of the history and geography of a particular city.

The problem itself, that of building within an urban pattern, generates direct questions about cities. Can they continue to grow as an expression of man's social instincts? Are they fixed statements requiring only polish, do they need to be reconstructed to accommodate major changes, or are cities no longer relevant? The entries added to these debates showing that young architects approach the city with constructive optimism.

The chosen sites for projects where public and private life meet, can be divided into two broad categories. The more flexible and organic the grid, the more routes and spaces are to be found. A rigid grid is less flexible and accepts changes in the life of the city with more discomfort. In gentle times the spaces between the blocks of private buildings are the public routes, yet with the advent of the motor car the routes are made inhuman.

The entries in the competition demonstrate three states of change. When material wealth is low or the land form varied, traditional routes are maintained. When the blocks are free forms within the grid, an independent pattern of pedestrian routes is threaded through. But when rigid blocks are set between a grid of roads filled with large motor cars moving at high speed, the possibility of interaction between the public and private life of the city is much reduced or even eliminated. Unhappily this is shown clearly in some entries and consequently the designers are not in the running.

Another group of entries is also excluded, though by a more deliberate decision of the authors. They did not submit real designs and have chosen to offer a vision of the city in imaginative images which offer a manifesto for the future. Much enjoyment is to be had in their work.

Very few of the designers play the role of weary professionals, and thereby have escaped the professionals' sin of knowing the rules to the exclusion of imaginative human responses. The best demonstrate the ability to see beyond the limitations of a site. They do not stop at the legal boundary but flow on to embrace the life of the city. They have understood the competition.

The competition attracted 419 entries, the work of 750 students who explored the problems of over 100 cities throughout the world. This positive response displays universal creativity which crossed national, political and economic boundaries.

'Where are the temples?' asked Courtenay Blackmore. Few of the competitors chose to add a temple whether of religious or social importance. This illustrates the modest ambitions of this generation of designers, which is perhaps a good thing for our future cities.

The discrepancy between the quality of the work of these students and that exhibited in the new building in our cities is emphasised by Sir Richard Rogers: 'The city is first and foremost a meeting place for people. It is the talent which comprehends that for which we were searching – and found. But where does the young talent go? There is so much here and so little out there.' *Denis Serjeant*

1st Prize: *Spencer Fung (below), Architectural Association, UK*
2nd Prize: *Ken Grix, University of Bath, UK*
Joint 3rd Prize: *Salomon Mosse, Danny Mintz, Israel Institute of Technology, Israel; Enrique Hermosa-Lera, Staatlich Hochschule fur Bildende Kunste, Frankfurt, Germany; Vyacheslav L Nickitin and Alex L Danchenko, Kazan Institute of Construction Engineering, Russia; Mathew Miszewski and Anya van der Merwe-Miszewski, University of Cape Town, South Africa.*
Judges: *Sir Richard Rogers, (opposite), Courtenay Blackmore, Denis Serjeant, Graham Stirk*

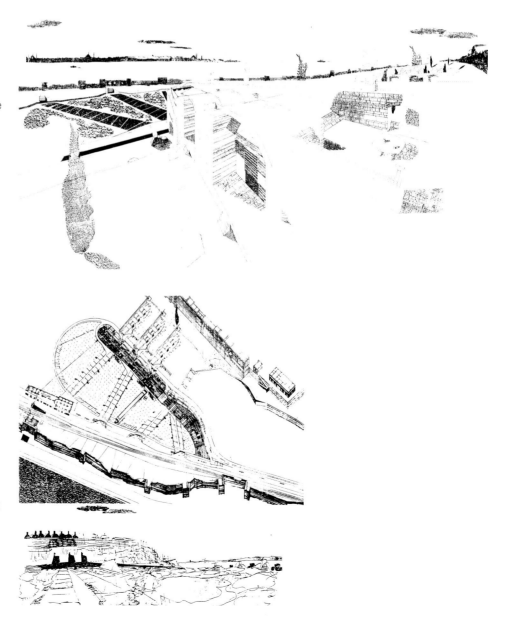

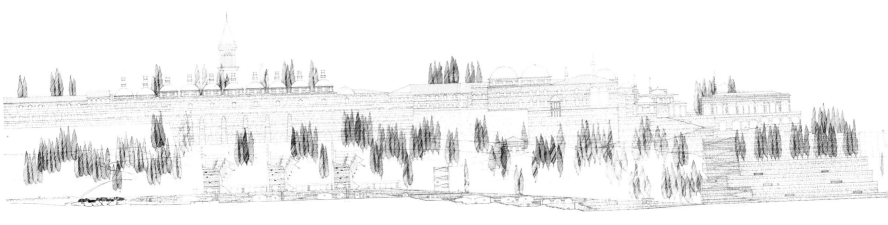

1st PRIZE
SPENCER FUNG
Architectural Association, UK
Caravanserai, Istanbul

Situated in Istanbul within the Topkapi Palace grounds, Spencer Fung's Caravanserai project embraces both the abutments upon which the impressive acropolis of Topkapi rises, and the coast by the Marmara sea where courtesans once enjoyed the sea breezes in pavilions and formal gardens. Thus the relation between old and new is a prime concern of the project. Using the device of a modern-day caravanserai, Spencer Fung has reconstituted the former relationship between the palace, now a museum, its grounds and the seashore. The site, which is now owned by the military and overgrown with weeds, reverts to its former existence as a pleasure-ground.

The project responds to certain features of the site: the 'buttress motels' seem to extend the foundations of the palace wall; railway hostels are placed along the railway lines in a manner analogous to the ancient sea-wall towers; entrance spaces to the caravanserai originate in archeological traces. Various categories of travellers generate a specific response in the project: hikers find shelter in open-air hostels; campers choose from random sites in extensive olive orchards; affluent motorists find more comfortable accommodation in motel apartments. A whole range of spaces is proposed – buildings, plinths, traces and gardens. The extensive infrastructure of drives, promenades, tavernas, communal kitchens, and public bathing-houses reads rather like the foundations of a city without the buildings. As the tents unfold, so the city acquires a distinct character. Trees cover much of the ground with the potent silhouette of Topkapi dominating from afar.

The proposed architecture is austere and heavy. Stone prevails, though fragile materials are combined with it to provide intimacy and the kind of pleasurable spaces to be expected from such a programme. The architectural language is clearly indebted to Ottoman architecture in this respect, although this is the result of interpretation rather than mimicry; roof-terraces, for example, recall Ottoman precedent, but also develop a modernist theme. *Rodrigo Pérez de Arce*

2nd PRIZE

KEN GRIX
University of Bath, UK
Public Baths, Valetta, Malta

This is a fine example of the extension and enrichment of a route that falls dramatically through steep gradients to the seabound edge of Valetta. Similar to the first-prize scheme in that it is a quiet, competent solution to the elements of the brief, it differs in that it expands the natural movement from the centre of the city outwards rather than impressing those arriving from distant lands. The change of level is enormous and most skilfully managed with ingenious mixes of public and private spaces.

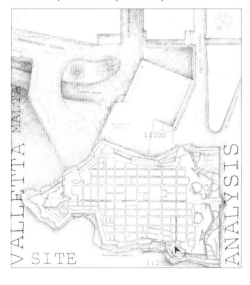

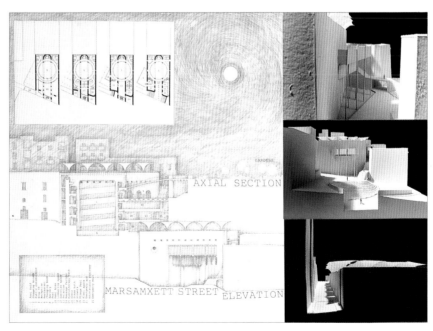

RECENT WORK

SPENCER FUNG
Otemon Apartment Building, Fukuoka, Japan, 1991

This scheme was the first-prize-winner in the Otemon Housing Competition for an apartment block in Fukuoka.

The form of the block arose out of the very strict constraints of its surroundings: an urban plot in a city with an active street life; with a north-facing frontage onto a noisy street and in a densely, irregularly gridded part of the city. On top of this were the restrictions of the municipality's overall height regulations and in particular the street frontage height regulations which constituted a problem of light penetrating into the site.

This was solved by a configuration of a court-garden flanked by a front and a lower rear southern block housing the apartments. This allows ample sunlight to reach all apartments. The court-garden, with the elements of water, plants and textured planes becomes the focal point for all the apartments. By raising the court-garden a storey above the street, and linking the two by a generous stair, enough privacy was created to allow a visual connection to the busy street through a glass foyer.

The duplex apartments are then entered via the foyer, and are arranged linearly in the front block allowing a flow of open space between north and south balconies. On the south privacy is maintained and light and shade are regulated by moveable louvred screens on the balconies. The apartments combine double-height living rooms on one side, with single-height bedroom zones above the dining and kitchen areas on the other. Sliding glass walls of the double-height living rooms and some bedrooms open freely onto the louvred balconies that control the flow of sunlight into the apartments.

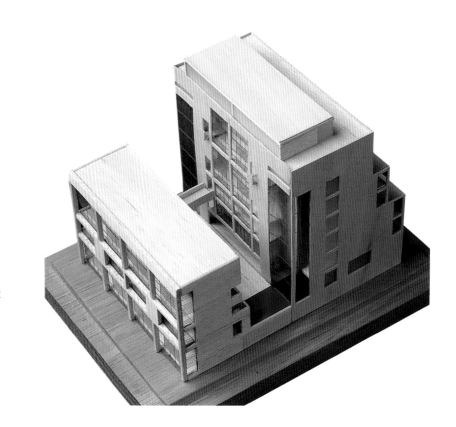

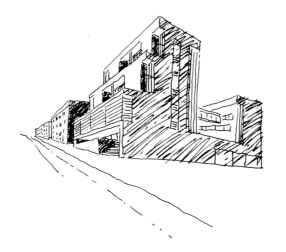

KEN GRIX
0=0+0

The relief 0=0+0 is a study of equivocal spatial shape. The complex unitary form of the relief is also understood as two inter-penetrating spaces of simple shape. The conception of unitary space is strictly founded upon reality, whereas the conception of two coupled spaces is structurally more imaginary.

The latter conception is shaped by the Gestalt perceptual criteria of simplicity, similarity and continuity. Both shapes are simple. The material surfaces of either space are related by simple stereometry and colour similarity. The imaginary surfaces of either space are continuous where the material surfaces are absent.

The conception of coupled spaces necessitates that the absence of material surfaces in the centre of the relief is held to be the result of either space occupying a part of the stereometric domain of the other. This is the phenomenon of spatial interpen-etration or mutual occupancy. The local structure of the phenomenon is purely imaginary, thus the observer may attribute dominance of occupancy to either of the spaces, or contemplate the existence of both spaces in the same place, at the same time.

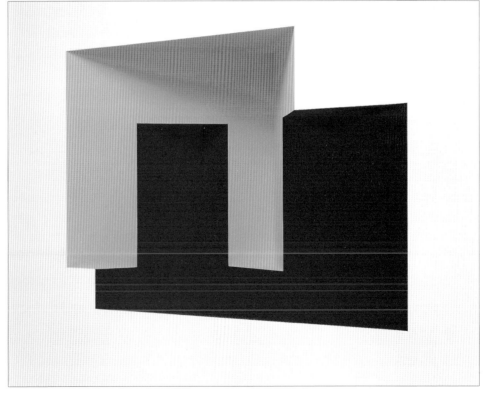

JUDGE
SIR RICHARD ROGERS
Tokyo Forum Competition
1990

After Beaubourg and Lloyds, it looked as if
that particular line of architectural enquiry
had reached a natural limit. There was
nowhere further to take the idea of served
and servant space. The Rogers office
began to move instead towards an exploration of the expressive possibilities of an
architectural language derived from Erich
Mendelsohn, but nonetheless the Tokyo
Forum looked like a development of the
ideas set out at Beaubourg.

As an architectural object, the project
would have had its biggest impact on the
side walls with three primary auditoria
projecting forward from the shelter of the
portal frames, reflecting their varying sizes.
The rake of the auditorium floor would have
been reflected in the form of the capsule
slung from the portal frame, with the
entrances from the top calling for a network
of snaking escalator tubes to carry audi-
ences up from the Forum floor.

Tokyo has the teeming street life and the
organisation to use such a space to the full,
yet to date none exists. Huge institutional
structures of this kind tend to be dominated
by blank, windowless walls, providing a
forbidding and anonymous exterior. The
Rogers strategy has been to avoid this as
much as possible by making the building's
parts explicit. The provision of facilities
encouraging a wide range of social activities in and around the building would have
blurred the distinction between inside and
outside and created an open and inviting
complex rather than a blank and intimidat-
ing one.

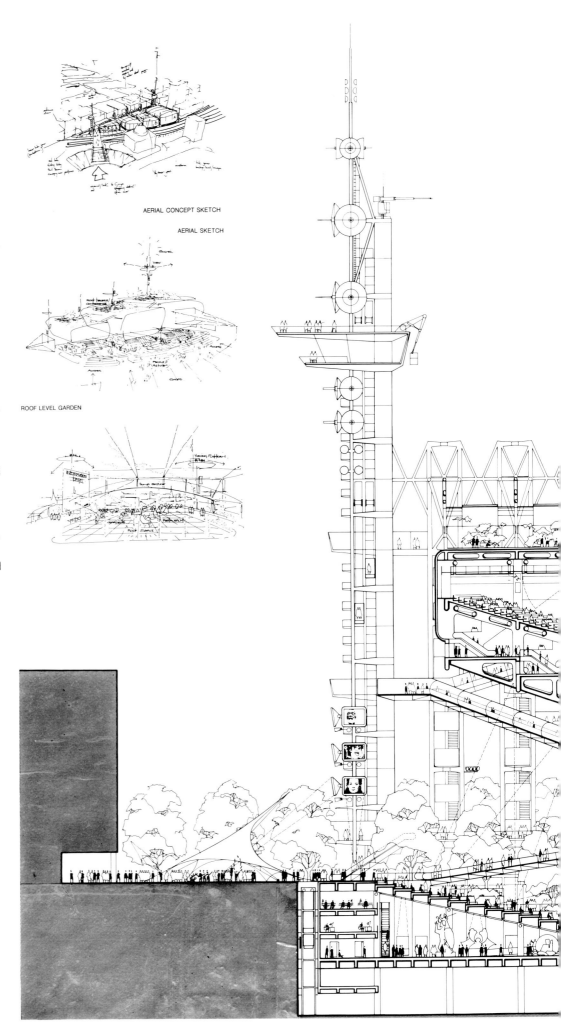

AERIAL CONCEPT SKETCH

AERIAL SKETCH

ROOF LEVEL GARDEN

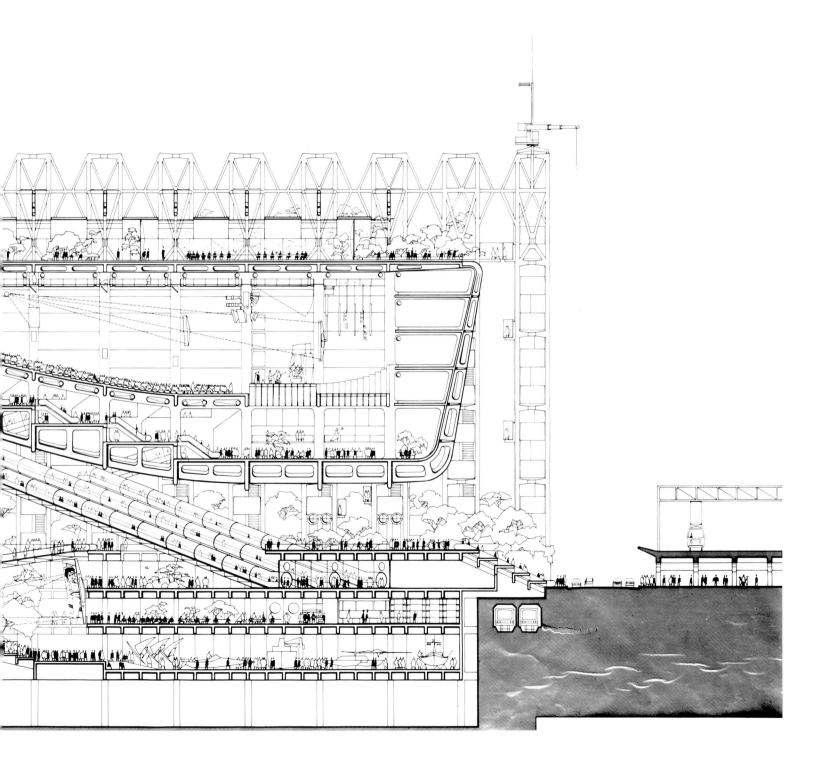

GASSTOP

The very banality of most oil company roadside architecture makes a gas stop a good subject for a student project. And the worldwide currency of petroleum makes it an especially apt choice for an international competition.

The typical standard gas stop is responsive neither to its site nor to anything but the most basic requirements of its users. The convenience of the oil company comes first, it is an inhospitable place where customers are hurried through rather than encouraged to linger and rest.

Derek Sugden's brief for the competition was to interpret the gas stop as a place of celebration – of arrival and departure rather than of the power and reach of a multi-national company.

The simplest strategy is to choose an unusual, sensitive, or spectacular site, using the building to focus the character of the place. A second possible strategy is to extend the brief. A few competitors focused on the mechanical basics: gas stop as vending machine or mobile service unit.

Because of this diversity of approach, the assessors decided to award four prizes. Two of the winning schemes, by Sim Meng Chu of the University of Strathclyde, and Timothy Hill and Antony Moulis of the University of Queensland, were chosen because they were the most accomplished works of architecture. Chandra Lee of the University of Natal and Mark Lecchini of Canterbury College of Art succeeded because of the imaginative way they combined two or more strategies – a mobile service unit with a social dimension and a dynamic response to an urban site plus a drive-in cinema.

The assessors were impressed by the range and quality of the entries, but there were some reservations. Services engineer Max Fordham found some of the more self-indulgent schemes hard to take: 'It seemed difficult to relate the fantasy to any kind of future reality.'

Derek Sugden's brief talked of 'the structural poetry . . . based upon an economy of means' and encouraged competitors to explore the possibility of a building system that would be adaptable to different sites and cultures. Very few,

however, seem to have been willing to compromise with economic realities or the requirements of a corporate client.

Sculptor Anthony Caro was suspicious of 'flashy drawings and nice little models'. Derek Sugden also suspected 'a conscious obscurantism in the drawings'.

Only Ted Cullinan seems to have been at home with even the most deconstructed presentations. Most fascinating of all to Cullinan were the entries by Chinese students struggling vigorously to recover an understanding of their cultural past.

There is a great deal to be learnt from an international competition such as this – and not only by the students who take part.
Colin Davies

Joint 1st Prize: *Sim Meng Chu (below), University of Strathclyde, UK; Timothy Hill and Antony Moulis, University of Queensland, Australia; Chandra Lee (opposite), University of Natal, South Africa; Mark Lecchini, Canterbury College of Art, UK.*

Judges: *Edward Cullinan, Derek Sugden, Sir Antony Caro, Max Fordham.*

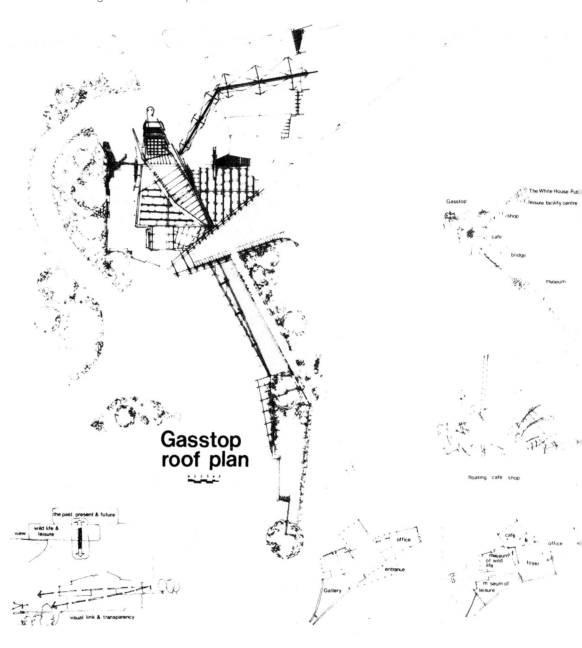

Gasstop roof plan

JOINT 1st PRIZE

SIM MENG CHU,
University of Strathclyde, UK
Maryhill Locks, Glasgow

The assessors chose this scheme for its
elegance, its sensitive response to context
and its excellent interiors: 'The designer
tackled the potential of a difficult place,
tackled it as if responding to a client's
wishes, and did it superbly. We were struck
by the sensitive feel for a complicated
working place, beautifully drawn.'

JOINT 1st PRIZE

MARK LECCHINI
Canterbury College of Art, UK
Metropolitan Pitstop

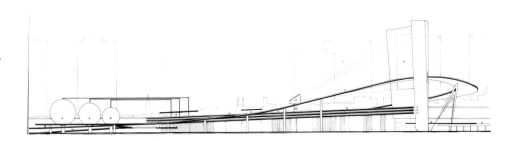

A playground for fuel-injected, turbo-charged car culture, sited between the Westway and Paddington Station. The assessors admired its vigour, its planning skill and its understanding of urban scale: 'Taking a very broad view, the designer got down to first principles, to the ideas of fuelling, resting and so on. It was really ambitious in this context and managed a convincing synthesis, drawn in an under-standable way.'

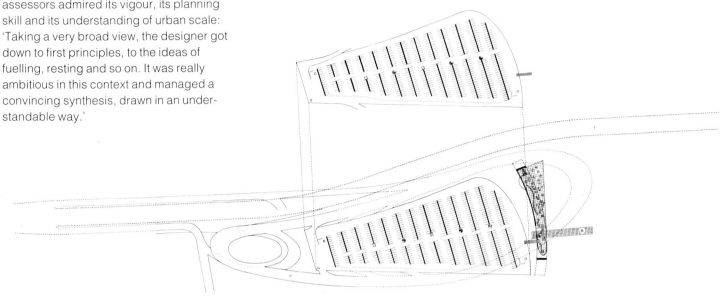

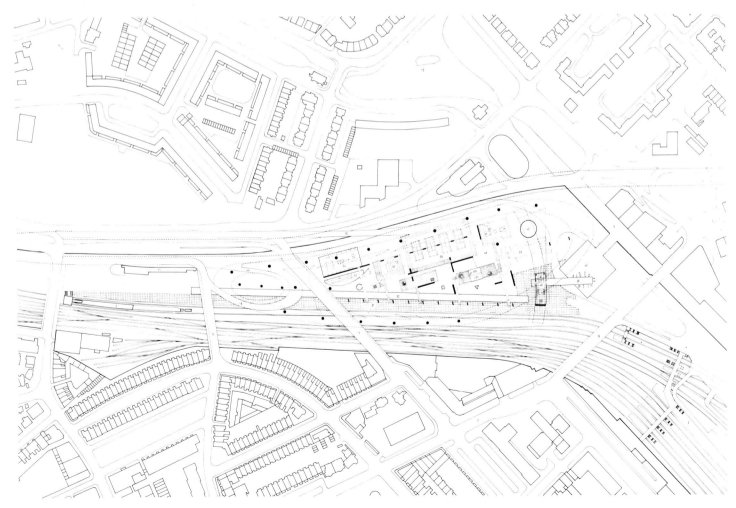

JOINT 1st PRIZE

TIMOTHY HILL AND
ANTONY MOULIS
University of Queensland,
Australia
A Tilt Up Fill Up

A gas stop high in the Great Dividing
Range, a 90-minute drive from Brisbane.
Once again the assessors admired the
sensitive response to context: 'The building
reacts to its site with great wit and delight.
The wit and delight, however, spring from
an unpretentious practical building where
the construction is elaborated to give
richness and to fulfil the complicated
functions of enclosure.'

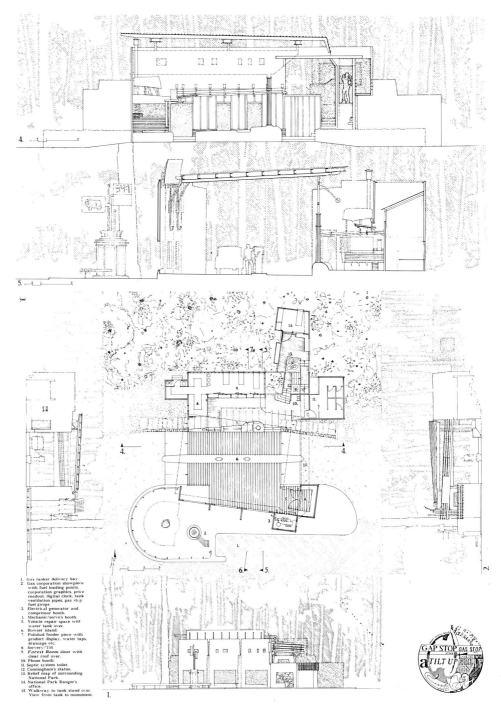

1. Gas tanker delivery bay.
2. Gas corporation showpiece
   with fuel loading points,
   corporation graphics, price
   readout, digital clock, tank
   ventilation pipes, gas step
   fuel gauge
3. Electrical generator and
   compressor booth.
4. Mechanic/servo's booth.
5. Vehicle repair space with
   water tank over.
6. Bowser island.
7. Polished fender piece with
   product display, water taps,
   drainage etc.
8. Servery/Till
9. *Forest Room* diner with
   clear roof over.
10. Phone booth.
11. Septic system toilet.
12. Cunningham's statue.
13. Relief map of surrounding
    National Park.
14. National Park Ranger's
    office.
15. Walkway to tank stand over.
    View from tank to monument.

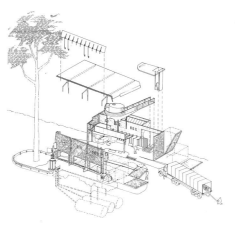

JOINT 1st PRIZE

CHANDRA LEE
University of Natal,
South Africa
Jabulani Gas Stops

Cheap petrol delivered to the township of Durban by a truck broadcasting music from its roof-mounted loudspeaker. The assessors liked the imaginative way the designers had tackled a vast urban problem: 'The truck, with its radical approach of taking fuel to the townships and then adding all the other activities which would develop in its wake, showed inventiveness and artistry. There are precedents for the technology in the design of aircraft bowsers.'

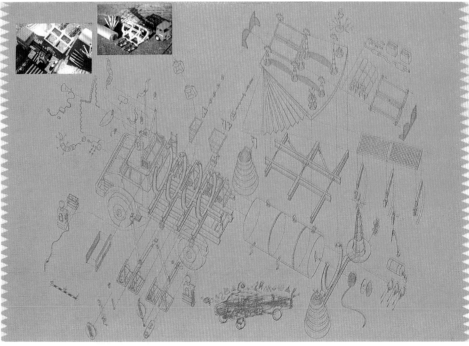

RECENT WORK

SIM MENG CHU
The Kelvin Museum of Industrial Archaeology, UK

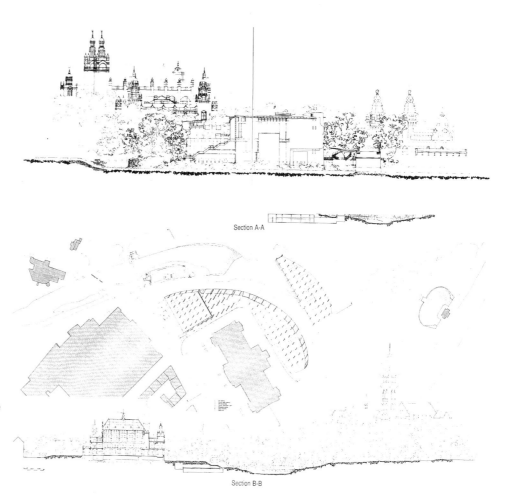

Section A-A

Section B-B

My main focus is on the Kelvingrove Park and the River Kelvin. It is to be developed as an industrial, residential and cultural area, all adding an urban richness to what has become one of the most significant areas of Glasgow. The Kelvin Walkway is a contextual walk which connects all the important events along the river and the park. My intention is to respond to the past and the industrial heritage of both the River Kelvin and the immediate area, and to provide a building as the terminus to the Kelvin Walkway.

The content and purpose of the material in the museum along the walkway provides an opportunity to preserve and interpret the heritage of the locality.

The journey ends with the cafe on the north side of the river offering a unique experience of looking back to the park, the river and the museum.

TIMOTHY HILL
Fortitude Valley House Additions

'The intriguing aspect of this building is the way it interweaves the interior spaces with the landscape of the rear yard, which was created to be a formal contemplative garden, unlike the traditional utilitarian Australian back yard.' *Ian McDougall*

'This inner-city suburban house attempts to be additive in the broad sense. It does not restrict itself to the original vernacular language and tests its pliancy by subordinating it to the ideality of the landscape. Exterior spaces function as landscape receptacles with the building fabric acting as an articulated crust. The plan distribution can be seen to have emerged from a detailed attention to patterns of usage coupled with an idea of fragmentation and an aesthetic of crisp, clean lines. Compositionally, the design continually seems to seek a balance between asymmetrical elements.' *Peter Besley*

ANTONY MOULIS
Medium Density Housing in Brisbane Intentions

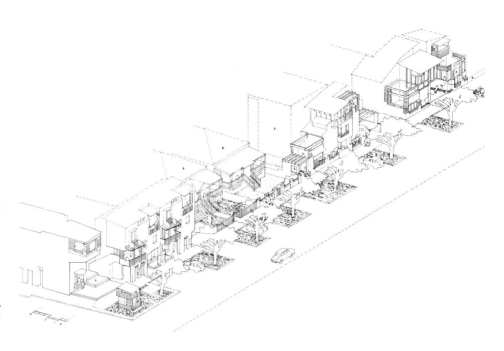

This project is about medium density housing in Brisbane. The main intention is to re-evaluate the street as 'a public room within the city' both spatially and as a place for urban life. In the links between rooms reside the narratives of community and domestic life.

Key strategies are those of infill and rehabilitation; for instance, apartments made within the six-metre building setback. Diversity is sought after, not only in terms of mixing uses (say, shops and dwelling) but of domestic patterns, working from home, renting adjacent self-contained space, living by yourself, patterns that exist within our cities.

MARK LECCHINI
Europan 2

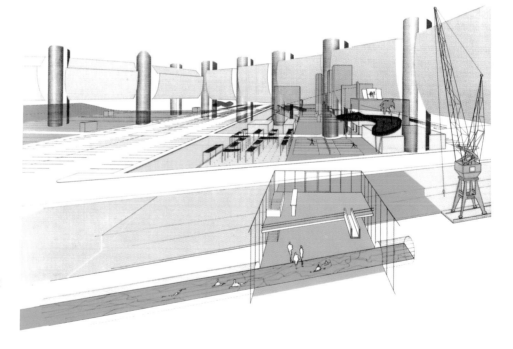

Cities squash events together and exciting mutations are squeezed out. This project has aimed for organised chaos, anarchy within a framework. Strips of activity run parallel from north to south. Within this rational pattern, associated facilities are scattered like confetti, dependent on the current demands and economics of the city. Each zone has its own programme. Sometimes these programmes interact across the strips. The terraced roof of a block of shops in the retail zone provides seating overlooking an all-weather, multi-purpose games pitch in the athletic zone. It also has a view across to the commercial zone where the curved wall of an office block acts as an outdoor cinema screen.

The housing is an entity in its own right. By floating over the strips, it ignores the rigorous diagram and can respond to the city's evolution within itself. It is stable with its vertical communication towers anchored firmly into the ground. Even the most anarchic personalities enjoy a safe refuge from the chaotic buzz of the city.

CHANDRA LEE
Shelter Durban Street School

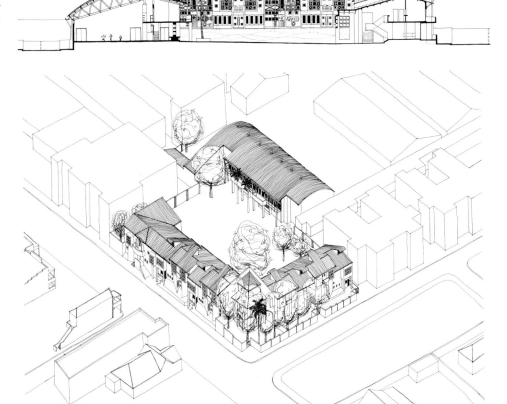

This development is based around a square to create an intimate and homely atmosphere. The enclosed space creates a safe area for recreation. The houses are set against each other to form an undulating surface, and the shadows that this creates lend texture and contrast to the overall appearance. The houses are imaginatively detailed with features such as balconies over the entrance to each house and overhanging sash windows echoed by smaller openings that pepper the surface.

JUDGE

EDWARD CULLINAN
Royal Opera House
Covent Garden
1983-84

We had three aims for the scheme; that it must present itself outward to the surrounding city along its own outer edges, that it must work inward from those edges towards and into the Opera House to allow it to work better, and that it established a new garden above, in which the fly tower could flourish.

Facing Outward

We proposed to re-assemble the combined elevations of the Bow Street and Covent Garden cast-iron facades of the historic Floral Hall next to the existing portico of the Opera House: for the Covent Garden side of the new Opera House, we re-established the building line and maintained the scale and proportions of the original design, to complete the piazza. In detail, our treatment was a tribute to Inigo Jones's original design and a response to the surrounding buildings as they stood. A recreated stone arcade formed a base for new elevations, of glass and enamelled steel, arranged in Inigo Jones's proportions. Above, hedges lined the leading edges of terraces and formal trees marked the corners of 'a garden' overlooking 'the garden'.

Working Inward

We suggested rebuilding and enlarging the stage, fly tower and back and side stages to international standards, and improving the foyers, while not altering the character of the auditorium. Shops and cafes enlivened the ground floor, and offices in the floors above formed the Covent Garden frontage of the building.

The New Garden

By placing flats for visiting artists on the side of the fly tower, the perennial problem of its bulky, vertical structure becomes an attractive pavilion in our roof garden.

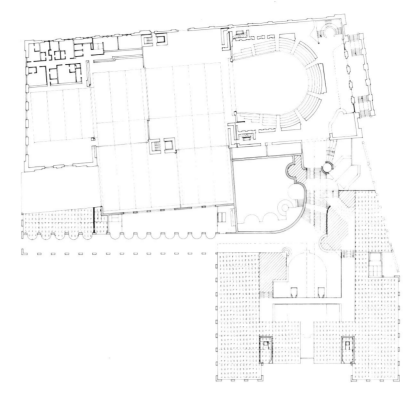

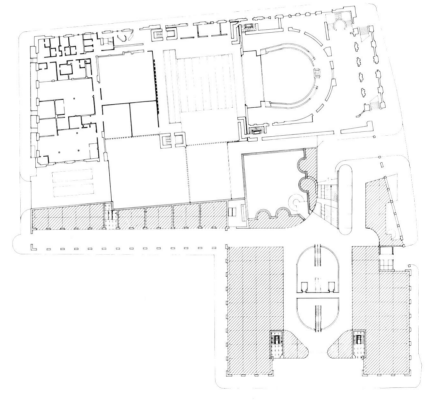

OASIS

Joint 1st Prize: *Elise Allison and Martin Feiersinger (below), Rice University, USA; Elizabeth Leung, University of Southern California, USA*
2nd Prize: *Sasa Randic, University of Zagreb, Croatia*
3rd Prize: *Weily Ran, University of Edinburgh, UK*
Judges: *Tadao Ando (opposite), David Chipperfield, Rodrigo Pérez de Arce*

Tadao Ando was not particularly interested in setting the standard competition problem of a specific building type. The conventional function of city architectural development is to make places for people in the context of wealth creation, he argued. But the speed of development we see at the moment raises the question of whether we should not be going in different directions: 'So instead of the idea of placing a building in the middle of a city I decided to investigate the city's peripheral areas to see what kind of things could be done there – to ask the students to pursue the problem from that position.'

Inevitably, the entrants focused on such problems as parking areas, motorways, railway yards, industrial sites – the planning detritus of modern cities worldwide. Their schemes were diverse not only in terms of the problems entrants selected and their design solutions, but in the level of thinking and imagination. The jury was looking for breadth and depth of thinking rather than for slick presentation or conformity to currently fashionable architectural styles.

The jury was surprised at the overall quality of competition entries. The best solutions represented the kind of thinking expected from experienced professionals, although that was tempered by the fact that in a student competition entrants should be exploring ideas to their limits.

Some students produced fascinating social ideas which were architecturally poor. A surprising number simply presented schemes straight from their course work. Others chose relatively easy problems to solve. And in some cases it was difficult for the jury to make useful comparisons because entrants concentrated on purely local problems and so it was impossible for them to judge the level of conceptual difficulty involved. That is an inevitable problem with international competitions but it is one which future entrants would do well to bear in mind.

The winners represented the best thinking from a very good set of the best. The jury was so impressed with two separate designs that they awarded an equal first. *Sutherland Lyall*

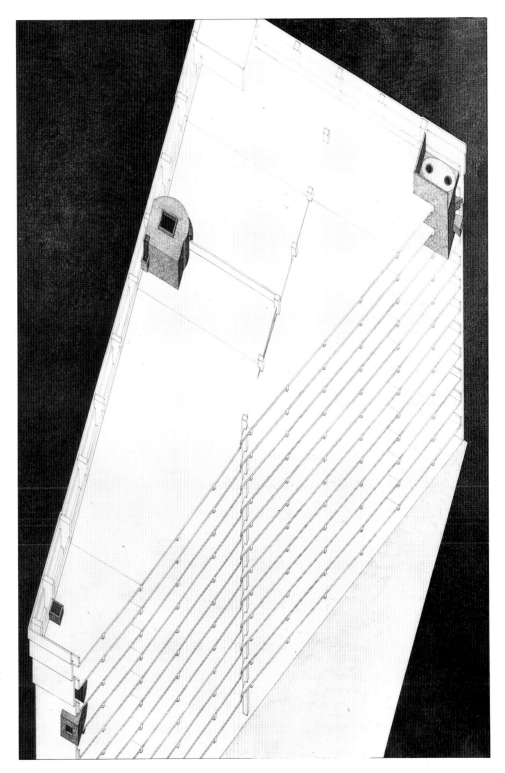

JOINT 1st PRIZE

ELIZABETH LEUNG
University of Southern
California, USA
Los Angeles Nunnery

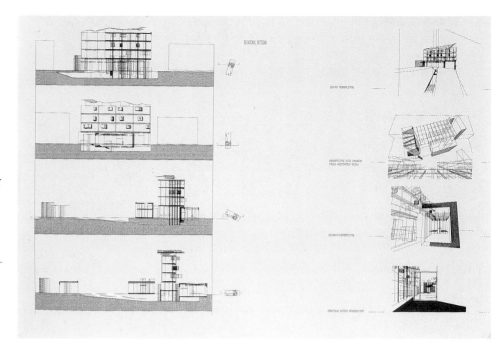

Leung's scheme is a monastery planned for a location on the industrial outskirts of downtown Los Angeles. The surrounding area represents desert, the monastery the enclosed oasis. The jury found the nesting levels of isolation in the design fascinating – the relationship between the outside world and the monastery enclosure, between the communal space of the chapel and the cells and the parallel relationship between the cells and the cells within the cells – in a sense a set of increasing intensities of isolation and solitude. Yet the primary view from within the monastery is of the skyscrapers of downtown LA – a metaphor for an emotionally sterile Babylon beyond the enclave's walls.

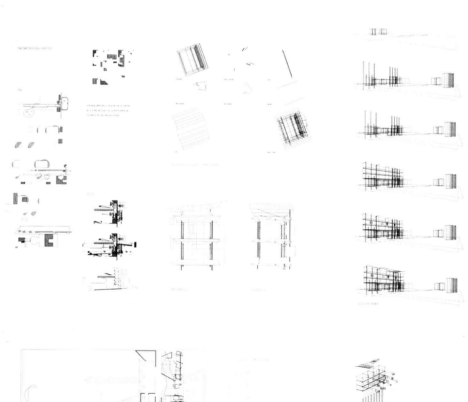

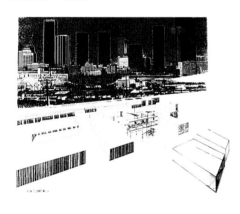

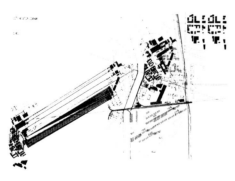

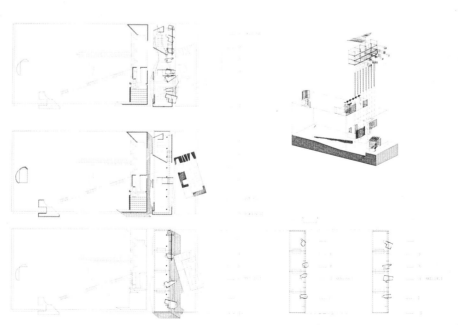

JOINT 1st PRIZE

ELISE ALLISON AND
MARTIN FEIERSINGER
Rice University School of
Architecture, USA
Houston Texas

This was a conceptually provocative scheme. Allison and Feiersinger pointed out that the idea of oasis implies the existence of a surrounding desert. Their project took a large car-parking building into which they inserted three cells. Each cell has the ostensible function of an observatory for viewing the skies, in a particularised way. For example, one is very heavily skylighted for contemplating the stars while another has horizontal windows for observing the setting sun. The cells exist in isolation from each other and although it is not specifically stated, occupants are presumably isolated from each other as well as from the city outside.

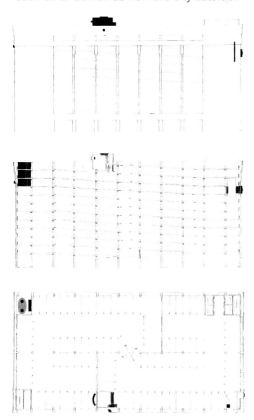

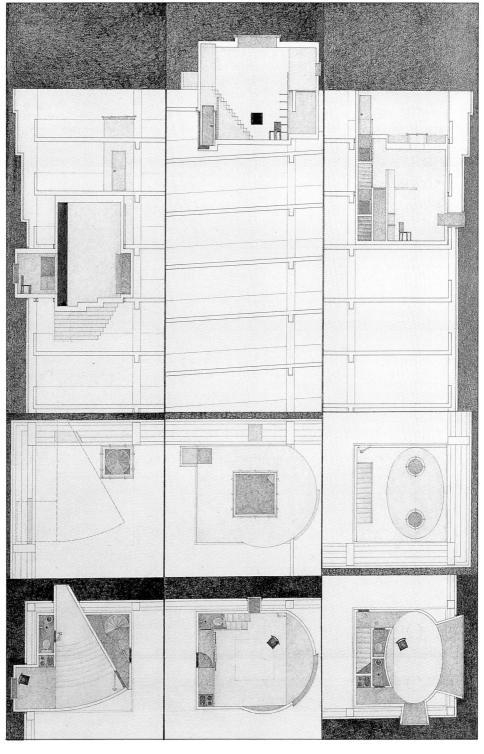

2nd PRIZE
SASA RANDIC
New Utopia

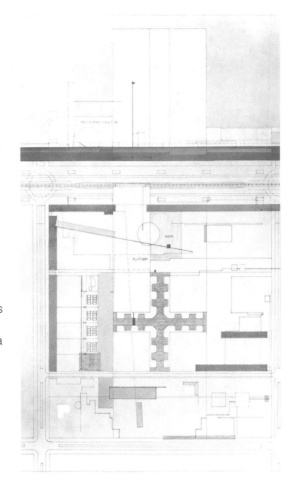

Randic argued that the most alienating city setting was not a motorway or an industrial landscape but the typical modern housing estate. The project has evolved as a critique of Le Corbusier's City of Three Million. At the urban level the project proposes a series of spaces which introduce social activity, qualifying the specific structure of the public areas of the City of Three Million. Building components are small apartments served by their own stairs and lifts which are parasitic on the Corb tower blocks. The jury saw the scheme as a metaphor for dynamic change – the revisions of a heroic theoretical architectural monument which represents the current changes in Eastern European political structures.

RECENT WORK
SASA RANDIC
Europan

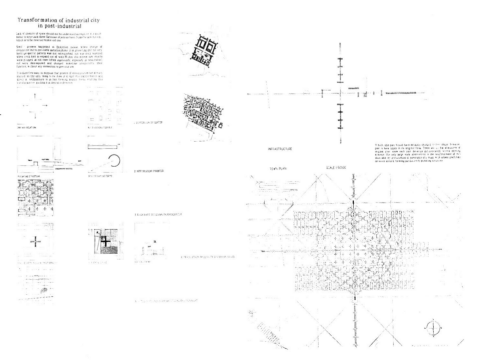

Demonstrating his philosophy that architecture is not about building, but about taking shape, Sasa Randic's 'Europan' is most notable for its Murano glass wall, which functions not only as a visual and sound barrier screening the total space, but disregards its immediate surroundings while reflecting the canal terrain by which it stands. Immense expanses of green are part of the design which links the historic town to the new. Housing a conference centre as well as an auditorium and other facilities, the 700 metre-long building transforms its own reality as well as that in which it exists.

ELISE ALLISON AND MARTIN FEIERSINGER
Europan II – Urban Gardens

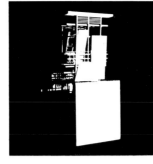

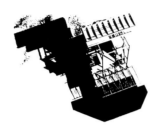

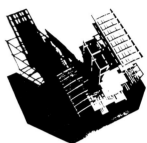

The 'autonomous individual', the 'individual in the group' and the 'individual in the midst of diversity' determine an urban concept which culminates in the definition of three zones and three distinct types of buildings.

Firstly, there is a concentrated zone, where houses with gardens and private garages interlace one with the other. The second consists primarily of public green spaces, edged with elevated loft-clusters. The three zones appropriate the same floor plan prototype: the usual living room is substituted by an indeterminate zone in the form of a long and narrow space alongside which all the service areas are placed. These compact rooms as one/two rooms with folding panels facing the 'free zone', allow one to co-opt the big space and also to retreat within. The filled rooms, as stations of the day, are minimal units as well as extensions of the indeterminate zone.

ELIZABETH LEUNG
Architecture as a Process of Reproduction

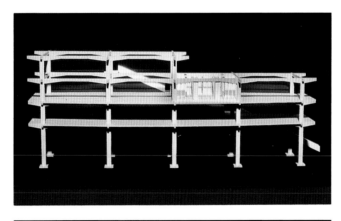

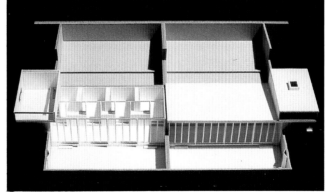

Architecture is the assimilated process of reproduction. Such juxtaposed parts form space. Therefore architecture is the art of making spaces.

The aim is to explore and develop a relationship between formal exploration of space and the investigation of reproduction as a process of making. There are three parts to the programme: conceiving, producing and receiving.

Due to the advancement of technological reproduction, this part seeks to explore how it affects our interior life. This is an investigation on the 'aesthetic', based on the industrial revolution.

This refreshes the challenge of Le Corbusier by exploring the relationship of machines to architecture. They demonstrate the variety, interdependence and indispensability of parts within a system.

Emphasis is upon the functional machine as an expressive system of parts and not just an efficient means.

JUDGE

TADAO ANDO ARCHITECT AND ASSOCIATES
JR Kyoto Station

The competition, commissioned by the Kyoto Station Building Development Co Ltd, West Japan Railway Company, was for a comprehensive mass-transit terminal in Kyoto, Japan's representative historical city, and a new urban centre for a 21st-century Kyoto, which would realise a new urban creation. The reconstruction project would involve the construction, on the present Kyoto Station site (approximately 3.8 hectares), of a new terminal building appropriate as a comprehensive terminal for 21st-century Kyoto and as a new sight-seeing spot in 'Kyoto of the world'.

Proposals for the basic plan of the entire site (including station, convention/hotel, and multiple commercial and cultural facilities), particularly proposals for a symbolic structure in the surrounding urban area, and an enriched space within the station concourse, were solicited.

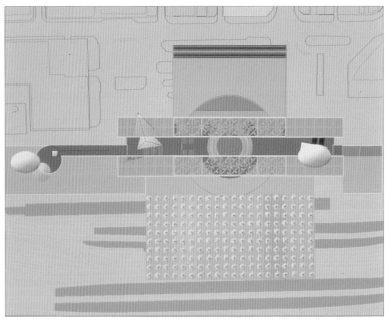

Design Summary by Tadao Ando Architect and Associates

A city is not brought forth out of utilitarian or economic reason alone. It has a multiplicity of values as a collective body of legacies amassed from history.

The creation of architecture means bringing to conscious life all that the vastness of time has concealed, and attempting a kind of catabolism within that historical context. Architecture must, in this sense, transcend its private aspect in order to function as structure for the city's public character and give rich life to city space.

In the name of economic rationality, the Japanese tradition of dwelling amid involvement with nature is being abandoned. By attempting to reunite the city with nature and history as they have been thus divorced, regathering what has become dispersed and bringing these into mutual dialogue, I seek to produce a new environment. This proposal symbolises this intent.

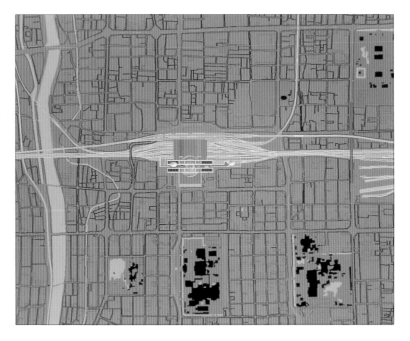

JUDGE
DAVID CHIPPERFIELD
The Museum of Scotland

In its role as principal partner, the existing museum dominates the new building, determining its very soul. The size of the 'extension' merits its own entrance, connected to the existing entrance hall. It is important that this 'internal' transition should be apparent to the visitor through a change of architecture. The new entrance is at pavement level, characterising the open nature of the museum and providing the complex with access for the disabled.

The proposal offers a critique of the existing museum and elaborates the possibilities that are offered by the juxtaposition. These include: accessibility, the provision of a large entrance foyer, flexibility, the control of daylight and the provision of 'external' spaces to provide relief from the exhibition floors. Behind the changing exhibits of the museum the building should provide a solid and architecturally pure shell, distinguishing it from other building types.

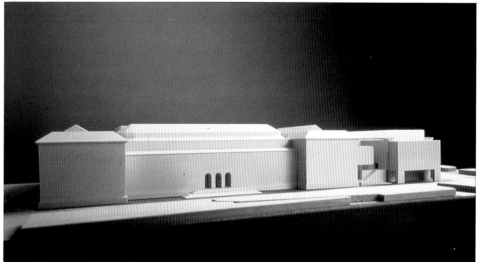

The monumental and civic programme of the museum forms the public elevations, while the more private library/administration block sits between the old and new, bridging the connecting axis, allowing the library to have its own entrance and facade. This split is elaborated by a cascading staircase, which leads to a courtyard on the south side and allows sunlight to penetrate into the north facing site. This stair doubles back, providing a final flight to the public restaurant and views over Edinburgh.

While the grand staircase provides relief from the main exhibition floors, a staircase next to the lifts provides a more direct link between floors, facilitating the circular routing of exhibition layouts. The main spaces are given a grain by the giant staircase and service piers, which also form small exhibition spaces along the edges of the main gallery spaces. The plan anticipates the exhibition spaces evolving to accommodate the collection. Main exhibition spaces are separated by a void from the external wall of the building, allowing daylight to percolate down the periphery of the building. Section, plan, structural services and daylight are woven together giving life to the building's perimeter.

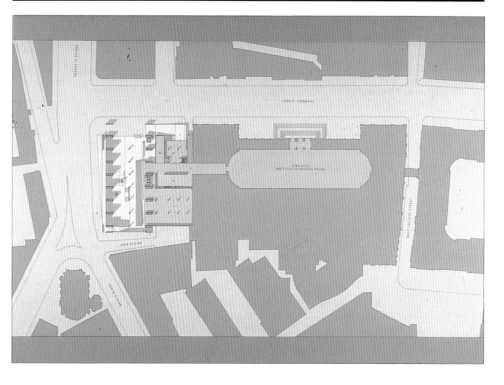

1990

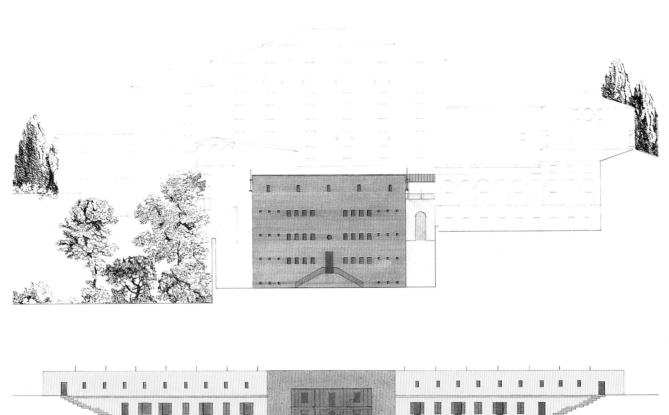

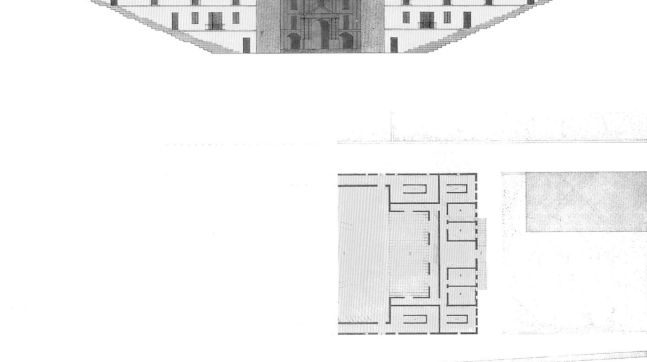

THEATRE:
A PLACE FOR ALL

'Architecture glorifies or immortalises something: where there is nothing to glorify there can be no architecture', wrote Ludwig Wittgenstein. These are brave words but in an age when the rhetoric of architecture has been so vilely traduced by the dictators from right and left it is a true test of imagination to seek its grounds in real situations. But certainly, there have been some political events (the breaching of the Berlin Wall; Tiananmen Square, Timisoara) that offered themes big enough to match such an ambition.

In the event the two quite outstanding schemes were of a more timeless nature, each recovering for an ancient town some ancestral memory and embodying it in the invention of new forms. These were exemplary cases in which research went hand in hand with novel thinking and thoughtful presentations of both form and argument.

There were a number of studies for a theatre but none of these promised a significant innovation. Generally, these proposals lacked a sense of a particular site or culture. Where the element of specific context was stressed the result was often a setting in which theatrical performance would have been frustrating.

The brief asked that the setting should be 'inviting to all sections of society', and this criterion led to the exclusion of a few ingenious schemes aimed at an audience of singular tastes.

Finally there were some interesting schemes celebrating phenomena in a broader landscape or natural setting. These schemes celebrated seasonal events and entailed a special trip for their enjoyment rather than the transformation of home ground in the city.

On the whole, it was a very refreshing display without domination by any fashion and mercifully unscathed by the promised resurgence of the Ceausescu style. There is inevitably the risk of some conflict between the nature of the subject of each competition and the subjects of study chosen within the curricula of each school. This tends to limit the submission of projects from those schools whose course work is more tightly structured and for this reason it is desirable that such topics should have an adequate level of generalness. What is particularly refreshing is the breadth of entry worldwide. This year's competition received 651 entries from 51 countries.

1st Prize: *Yen Ming Huang (top), Graduate School of Architecture, Taiwan*
2nd Prize: *Paolo Berca and Anna Maritano and Cesare Piva (opposite and bottom), Polytechnic of Turin, Italy*
3rd Prize: *Michael Lieb, Architectural Association, UK*
Judges: *Colin St John Wilson, Sam Wanamaker and Rolfe Kentish*

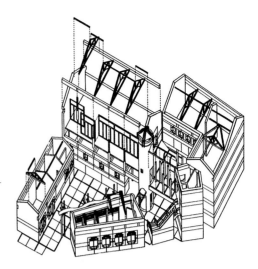

1st PRIZE

YEN MING HUANG
Graduate School of
Architecture, Taiwan
Historical Gate

In the case of the project for Tainan, the oldest city in Taiwan, the conceptual level is remarkably high. Three sets of ideas are interlocked with a view to 'revitalising the past to frame the present'. Time is represented by the withdrawal of the river from the heart of the city so that what was an important geographical feature has now become transformed into an important historical feature. The location of this event is qualified by three kinds of physical intervention – conservation (of two temples, a tower, a gateway, the site of the absent river), reconstruction (a tower, 'river-bank', flagpoles, bridge, West Gate of Tainan) and enhancement (the introduction of shops, residences and the activity centre). These 'theme-events' and their 'space-time' intersections are then reviewed in terms of four categories of 'framing' as the play between element and space alternates in terms of their relevant degree of focus. The thinking here is subtle – certainly it takes the consideration of space and time a long way beyond the conventional trite analogy to relativity. Unfortunately the building elements proposed do not match the level of the conceptual originality, but nevertheless they sustain the basic ideas well enough to assure this remarkable project its right to first prize.

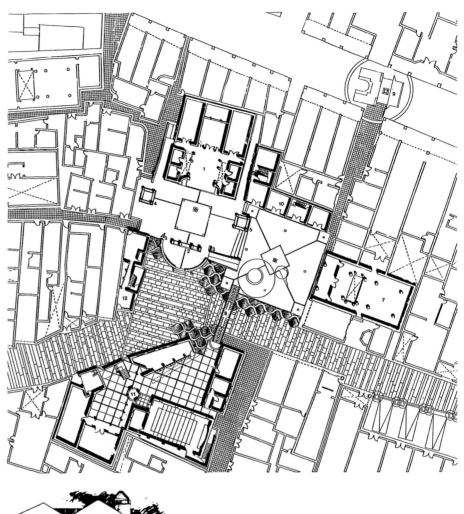

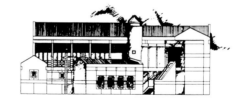

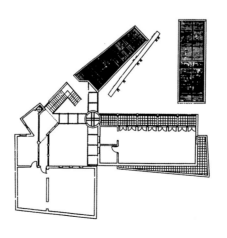

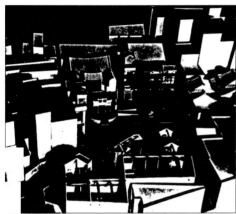

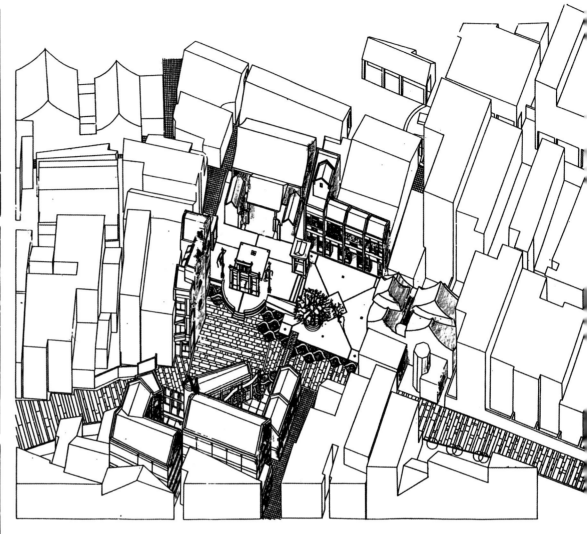

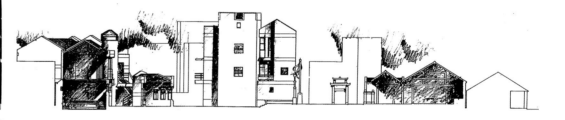

PAOLO BERCA,
ANNA MARITANO
AND CESARE PIVA
Turin Polytechnic, Italy
Saluzzo

The reinstatement of a historic theme has been used in this project as the spring-board for a beautifully developed invention. In the town of Saluzzo the old *loggia* depicted (in the *Theatrum Sabaudiae*) as enclosing the town square adjacent to the Savoy Palace Court is reinstated and becomes the entrance screen to a large outdoor theatre whose surrounding walls it embraces by extending along the two lateral facades. The theatre takes the form of an open-air auditorium, high walled and with a steeply raked auditorium confronting a *scena frons* in which the old town gate is recreated in wood behind the proscenium arch. The flank walls are wittily interpreted as conventional town elevations replete with balconies and windows, thereby restoring what might have been a heavy monumentality to the lighter urbanity of a typical Italian street scene. Here every detail reinforces the basic idea, the explanation is lucid and the draughtsmanship very beautiful. Our one reservation (which reduced it to second place) was that its basic *concetto* is a convention rather too often rehearsed in the Rationalist mode.

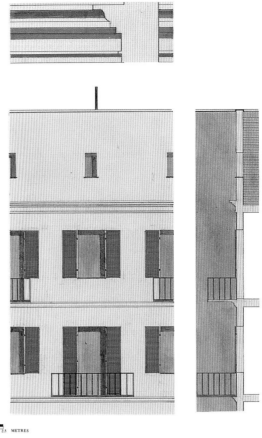

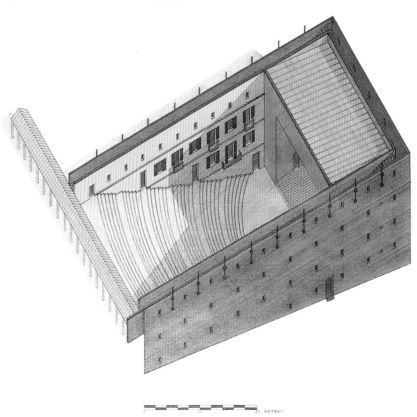

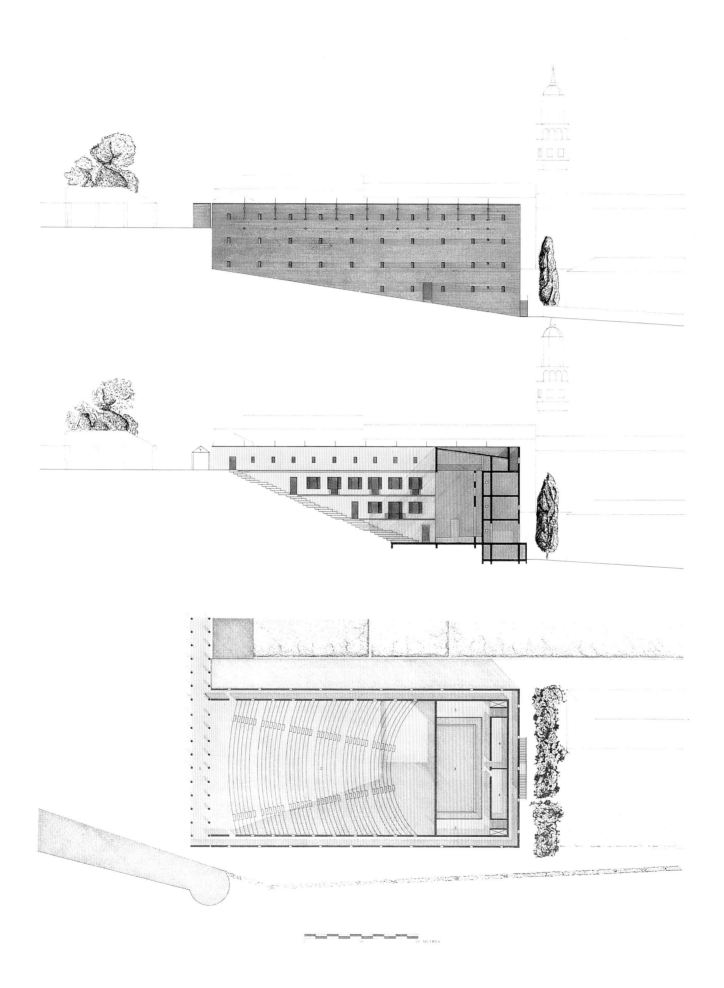

RECENT WORK
YEN MING HUANG
Design School

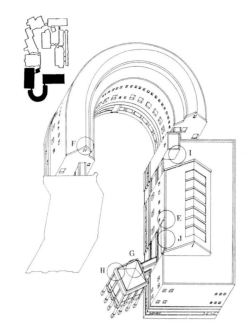

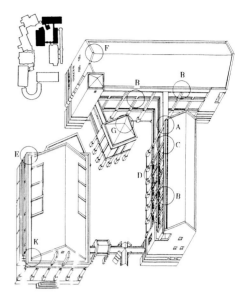

Examples that can teach us about the qualities of space and the methods of construction are also the fundamentals from which design competence can be built. Spatial examples are innumerable, but the spatial volume of the school is limited. To incorporate this idea into the design school, typological constructions were used as the 'example'.

I use columns and walls as the primordial materials to build my typologies. The spatial characters of the type develop as it is constructed. The functional assignment is of course based on its spatial characters, but the type *per se* does not preclude its possible uses. Individual types can also be organised in a compound structure to fit particular use requirements. Once all needed types are made and ready to be placed in site, there are spatial articulations concerning their positional relations as well as material modulations concerning their physical connections to consider. To use types is as much a creative act as to use words. Design in this case is not unlike poetic composition.

PAOLO BERCA
House for Artists

These drawings exhibit an idea, and they are an exploration of possibilities that when formulated try to establish a programme. They project and define an architecture of limits, which have always been established between environment and structure. Here the environment is imaginative or dreamed and is therefore a frontier of hope formed by the expectation of profitable meetings. Since time began we see it as a place of endeavour, of adventures, of horror, of meetings; of obscure perpetual liquid movement; of consecutive stratifications of water overlapping, interchanging according to mysterious rules. The sea has often united disparate people. Here the house is the only inhabited place and its relation to the environment as well as the relation between land and sea presents us with these architectural themes.

JUDGE

COLIN ST JOHN WILSON
Towards a New Cathedral

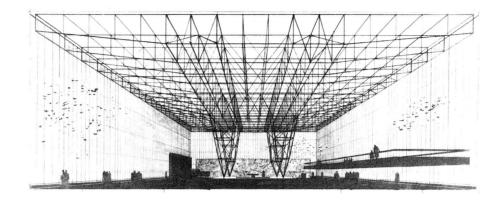

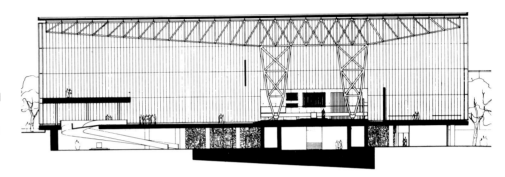

My choice of project was the open competition for Coventry Cathedral of 1950-51, which was close in spirit to the subject set for this year's competition.

I submitted a scheme with Peter Carter at a time when we worked together in the Housing Division of the LCC Architects' Department. I was reading Wittkower and *The Way Beyond Art* by Alfred Dorner, a highly volatile mixture of opposing forces; the possibility of fusing the extremes of technology with the demands of the sacred was very exciting. Wachsmann's space-frame studies for aircraft hangars offered a technical line of approach, but this was soon dominated by the demands of symbolic form, divine geometry, patterns of ritual, sense of occasion. Thus the composition was as follows:

1 The 'Chapel of the Resurrection' was enclosed within a tomb-like concrete cube, forming the platform for the altar.

2 The nave of the cathedral was at an upper level and approached by a ramp that encircled the place of enactment of the first of the Church's rituals – the baptismal font.

3 At the four corners of the altar platform there sprang four giant space-frame columns that in turn fused with the vast cantilevered space-frame of the roof. The cantilever from the entrance ramp on the west to the altar was of the order of 40 metres, from the altar eastwards over the Lady Chapel 20 metres and symmetrically to north and south on either side of the altar 17 metres. On arriving at the head of the ramp the impression of a vast tree-like canopy springing from the altar platform would have been overwhelming.

4 From the rim of this structure a curtain of glass and polished aluminium louvres was suspended. The blades of the louvres were so oriented that the view of the celebrants facing towards the altar would be closed by a shimmering veil of entrapped light: however, on turning to leave, the congregation would be presented with a sudden opening up of the walls to offer a full view of the world outside. And so light, structure and spatial experience would have been one with the meaning of the building itself.

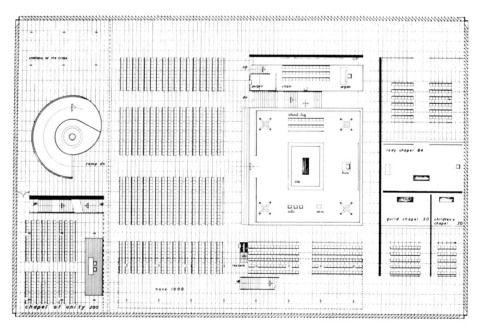

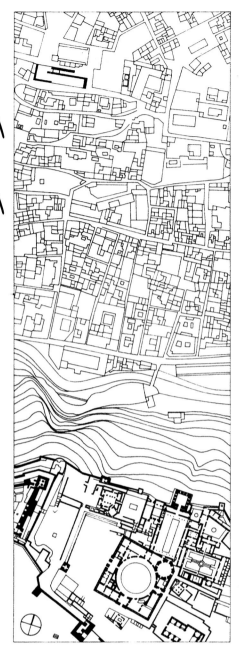

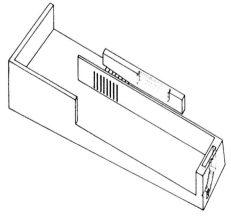

MONUMENT AND COUNTERPOINT

Joint 2nd Prize: *Stephen Harty (below),
Bartlett School of Architecture, UK; Matthew
Yeoman, Oxford Polytechnic, UK*
Judges: *Alan Stanton, Paul Williams, Alvaro
Siza Vieira, Jose Paulo dos Santos*

There was a consensus of opinion among the judges that many of the entries did not fully satisfy the brief's intent. Some projects were developed in a conventional and literal way but often lacked a strong conceptual base, others with stronger ideas tended to be less well thought through.

The winning scheme answered the spirit of the brief and followed its concepts through, but also conveyed tremendous personal conviction. Francisco Arevalo Toro, José Martín García, Juan Manuel Izquierdo, Yolanda Elena Latre Vegas and Marcos Pérez Monje's 'Mirador in Granada' was a unanimous winner of outstanding qualities. The sense of openness enables its subject, the Alhambra, to exist both within and outside the building. It is therefore not only an exhibition space for the Alhambra itself but is also designed for other activities, temporary exhibitions etc. The importance of the Alhambra in Arabic culture is addressed and respected. The building achieves its strength through its simplicity, and embodies a full awareness and integration of light. The project develops its ideas of time, space, atmosphere and topology yet resists the temptation to overcomplicate.

The judges decided to create an equal second prize. Stephen Harty's 'No Man's Land' is a highly conceptual piece of work which makes an extremely strong statement. Matthew Yeoman's 'Artist and Concept', while more conventional, pays great attention to detail and manages to use the brief to make an interesting and well developed project. It exploits the intrinsic aspects of the site and creates an interesting system of movement and spaces.

The three pieces of commended work were chosen for their ideas and strength of conviction, but it was felt none of the three went far enough.

In all, 500 projects were received from 39 countries, works which revealed the variety of current student work.

1st Prize: *Francisco Arevalo Toro, José Martín García, Juan Manuel Izquierdo, Yolanda Elena Latre Vegas and Marcos Pérez Monje (opposite), Escuela Tecnica Superior de Arquitectura de Madrid, Spain*

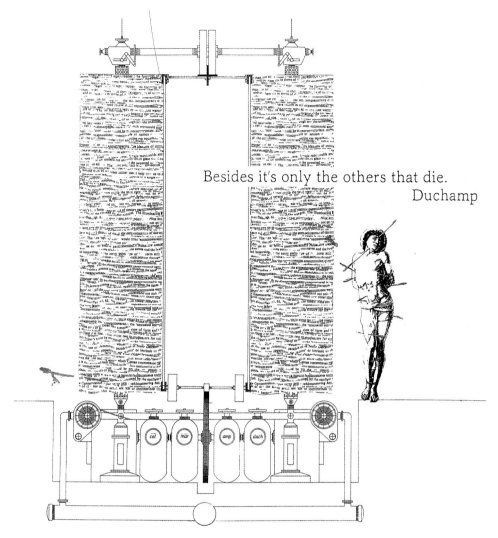

Besides it's only the others that die.
Duchamp

1st PRIZE

*FRANCISCO AREVALO
TORO, JUAN MANUEL
IZQUIERDO, YOLANDA
ELENA LATRE VEGAS,
JOSÉ MARTÍN GARCÍA AND
MARCOS PÉREZ MONJE*
*Escuela Tecnica Superior de
Arquitectura de Madrid, Spain*
Mirador in Granada

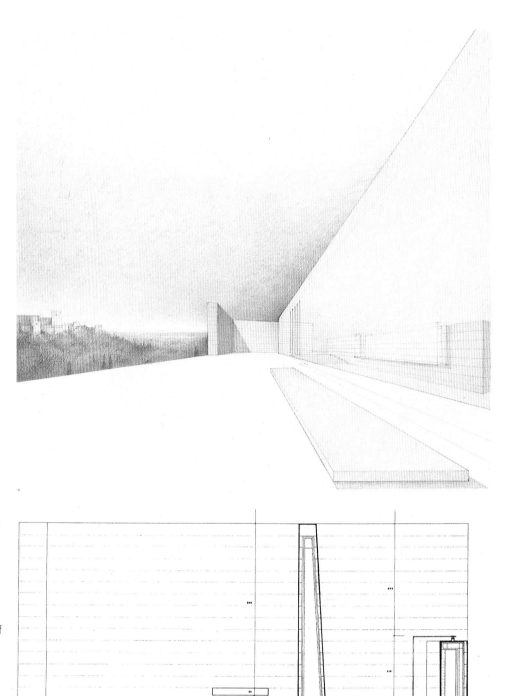

CONSTRUCTIVE SECTION

Granada, artistic and cultural site of
Spanish history, is the result of an encoun-
ter between two civilisations which melted
together. The walls of La Alhambra express the peak location of this tension.

The project is located in the 13th-century
Nazaries, Granada, on the Alcazba-
Cadima Hill in the Albaycan. We have taken
as the fundamental basis of the project the
continuing presence of La Alhambra, and
the idea of defining spaces which clearly
and explicitly enter into dialogue with our
understanding of architecture.

Mirador is configured by three walls that
articulate the space on the inside as well as
on the outside. The first wall is in an as-
cendant path which defines the principal
characteristics of the Mirador, being cut off
by a horizontal plane extending towards La
Alhambra. The massive wall that marks the
entrance is the exhibition space, with a
pure glass box where English engravings of
La Alhambra are exhibited. You walk
through the exhibitions between this wall
and another inclined one whose height and
position have been calculated to protect
the pictures from the direct sunlight. This
last wall is perforated at the end to evoke La
Alhambra in a sequence of tiered views that
anticipate the impressive scene that will
open up in front of us. The chosen materials
intend to continue the contrast between the
surfaces of the walls and the horizon from
which they emerge. The pavement is made
of white marble, and the walls of limey
sandstone that with the passage of time
takes a reddish patina.

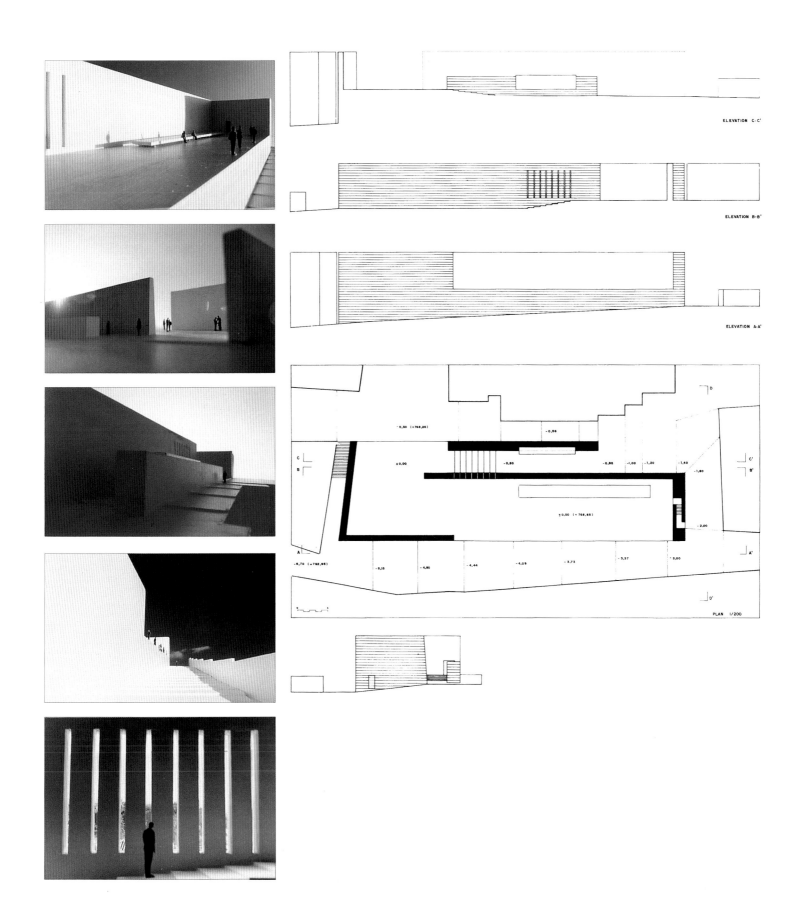

ELEVATION C-C'

ELEVATION B-B'

ELEVATION A-A'

PLAN 1/200

JOINT 2nd PRIZE

MATTHEW YEOMAN
Oxford Polytechnic, UK
Artist and Concept

Monument and counterpoint; the concept of duality; between light and shadow, transparency and opacity, heaviness and weightlessness, materiality and ethereality, form and spirit. The idea of unity of the opposites. The new counterpoint reinforcing the presence of the existing monument (Magdalen Bridge). A close accord exists between the natural element and the architectural one – in the interplay of open and closed spaces, transitions and contrasts, geometry and irregularity. A reverence for nature, for simplicity and spirituality and for reading objects in order to perceive the essence of things. The aim, to create a 'complex simplicity', evocative of the qualities inherent in the sculptures exhibited.

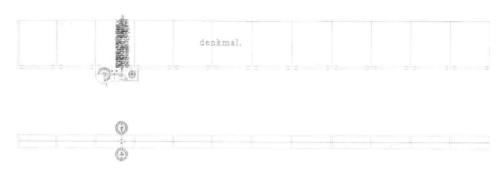

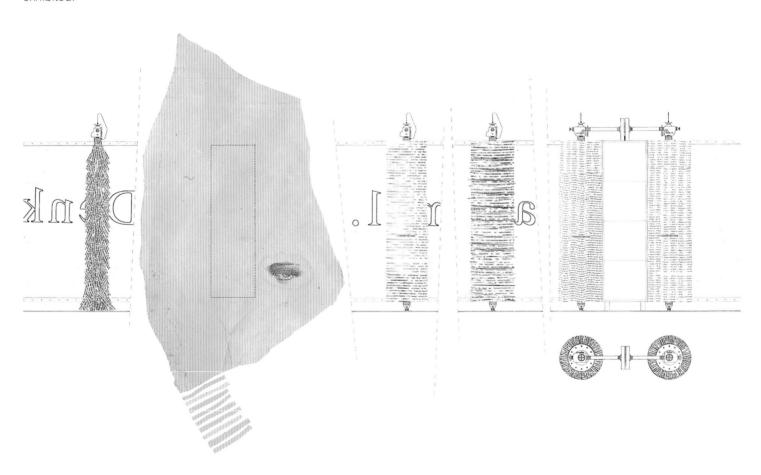

JOINT 2nd PRIZE

STEPHEN HARTY
No Man's Land

1 The site had everything and now it has nothing

1 The site had nothing and now it has everything

1 Architecturally vacant

1 Culturally loaded

1 The site (word) attracts meaning

1 Meaning is seen to be transitory and cultural rather than universal and natural

1 The past is a construction in the present

1 The past is temporary

1 Is not the most erotic part of the body (the city)

Where the garment gapes (no man's land)

It is this flash which seduces, or rather:

the staging of an appearance as disappearance . . . Barthes.

1 Duchamp's critique on the emptiness of sight

1 Location of Duchamp as opposed to Daimler-Benz reproportionalises conception of the absurd

. . . no man's land

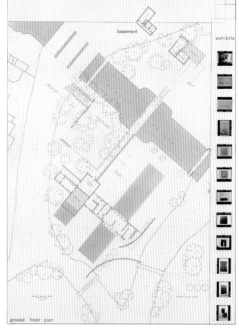

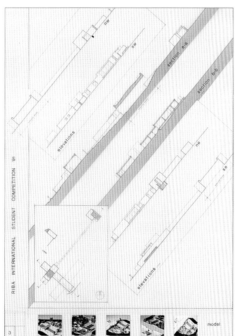

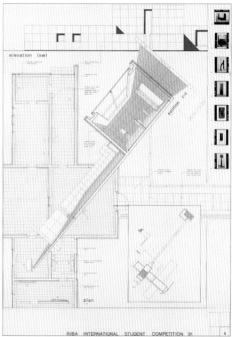

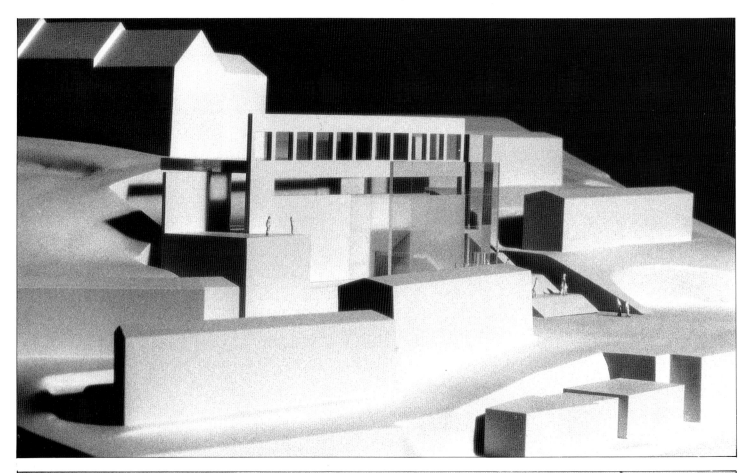

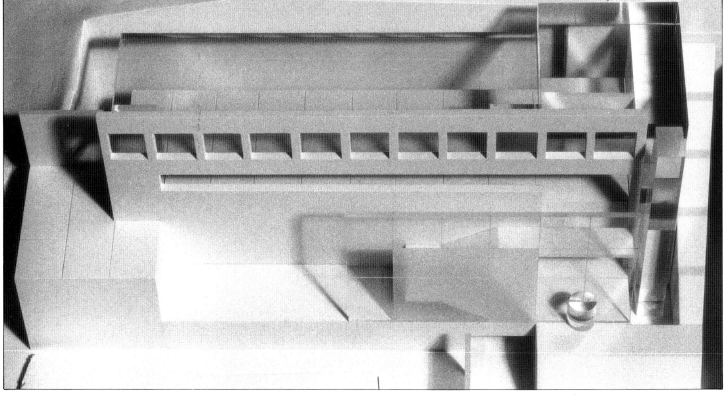

JUDGE
STANTON WILLIAMS
ARCHITECTS
St Ives Gallery

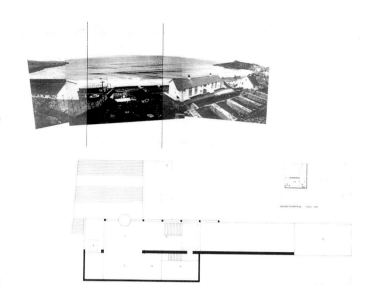

In November 1989 Stanton Williams
Architects were invited by Cornwall County
Council to submit a conceptual design
approach for an art gallery. The objective
was to create a gallery primarily for the
exhibition of Cornish paintings, drawings
and sculptures owned by the Tate Gallery,
together with space for educational activities and temporary exhibitions. The works
are mostly by painters and sculptors of the
St Ives School executed during the period
1939-75. The site was the old Gas Works at
Porthmeor beach in St Ives.

The brief asked for gallery exhibition
spaces; education and documentation
rooms; staff offices; workshop and storage;
shop; cafe; circulation and plantroom.
These were to be accommodated within a
total floor area of 743 metres square.

The building is developed from a series
of beautifully lit spaces for the pictures and
sculpture, and from the promenade through
the gallery. Conceptually, the building is a
series of vertical screens moving back from
Beach Road to the hillside. The outer
screen is transparent to make the building
as accessible and active as possible and
the inner screens provide a zone of protec-
tion for the paintings and sculpture.

The gallery is conceived as a simple and
flexible space. The configuration of walls
may be easily modified.

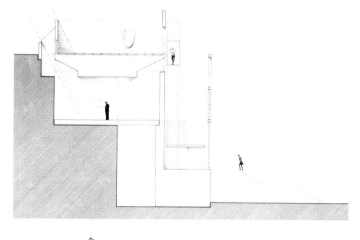

Externally the building extends the public
area of the street and beach with its terraced 'piazza'. A glass-enclosed lift, sited
at the corner of the building, will be visible.
The transparent facade allows people to be
seen moving up and through the building.
The cafe and sculpture terraces will be
visible from the beach and pavement. The
screen facades of the building will also
provide support for banners and exhibition
graphics. At night, the translucent and
transparent walls, glowing with light, will
animate the building.

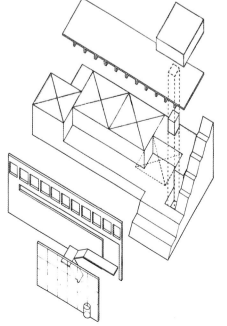

1992

HYBRID AND SUPER-IMPOSITION

The intention of this competition was to challenge the preciousness with which existing or historical conditions have been treated in the past. The brief aimed to challenge and violate the old orders to varying degrees chosen, identified and substantiated by the competitor.

The dictionary defines a hybrid as the offspring of different species; of mixed origins; a composition of incongruous elements. In an architectural context then, a hybrid or superimposition can exist in many guises, and that is what the competitor is to consider and respond to, no matter the location or activity.

The competitor may choose to design a hybrid building or superimpose, overlay or overlap one city plan with another. After all, there are hybrid cities and building extant around the world.

The important starting point was to impose the new hybrid upon an existing condition: there had to be a context, not necessarily urban, but rural or suburban; it might be in the form of a small scale within a much larger city context. Whatever the form, the chosen superimposition need not be onto a historical condition.

The hybrid could be superimposed at a different or conflicting scale to the chosen condition or location. This insertion could take the form of a new vertical order upon an existing horizontal order in two- or three-dimensional form.

The new hybrid could be a new system or programme implanted onto or into another, different system. One overall scheme can be composed of many different plans or sections superimposed or layered.

A new overlay or shadow may in fact be the only trace of the new upon the existing. It may not be physically visible at all. This then, is the one extreme to which the violation can exist.

The projects could work on a wide range of scales from city to detail, centre to fringe, domestic scale to city-wide.

To summarise, the superimposition of any of the following upon/into/on/through each other could result in an architectural hybrid:

horizontal
vertical
small scale within a large
  city context
archeological site
city scale
small scale to large scale
urban to rural
one system upon another

1st Prize: *Taku Shimizu and Giovanni Botello, Pratt Institute, USA*
2nd Prize: *Jonathan Buck, Polytechnic of Central London, UK*
Joint 3rd Prize: *Young J Yoon, Pennsylvania State University, USA; Nataliya Maximova, Dilara Zinatulina, Svetlana Nasretdinova, Svetlana Rasuleva, Regional Design School, Bashkirsky Dom, Russia, assisted by Elina Barykina, Mariya Balahontseva, Ildar Baikov, Iliya Litvinov, Varvara Sokolova, Vera Semyonova, Tagir Galiev, Veronika Zykina*
Judges: *Zaha Hadid, Christine Hawley, Itsuko Hasegawa*

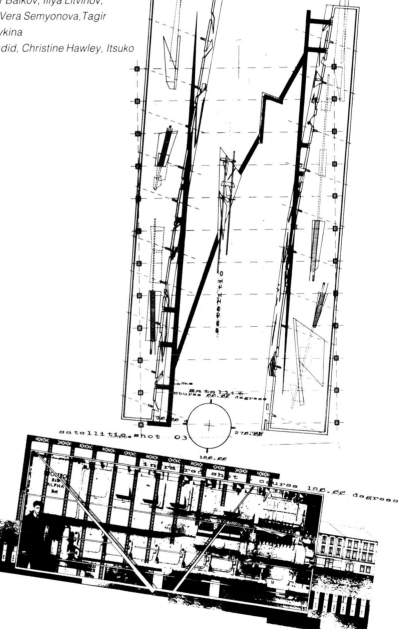

1st PRIZE
TAKU SHIMIZU AND GIOVANNI BOTELLO
Pratt Institute, USA

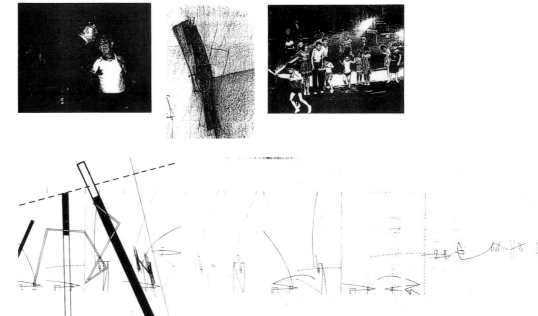

The aim of this proposal is to clarify the specific details and characteristics of two seemingly unrelated events by observing the physical, bodily movements of the unaimed yet temporal participants of the tea ceremony, and those of the specific yet unrehearsed persons of the street, recording their distinguishing movements, and hybridising such characteristics at moments of similar gestures. The resultant hybrid will begin to establish a specific temporal and spatial order to the seemingly fragmented events which characterise the present condition of New York City.

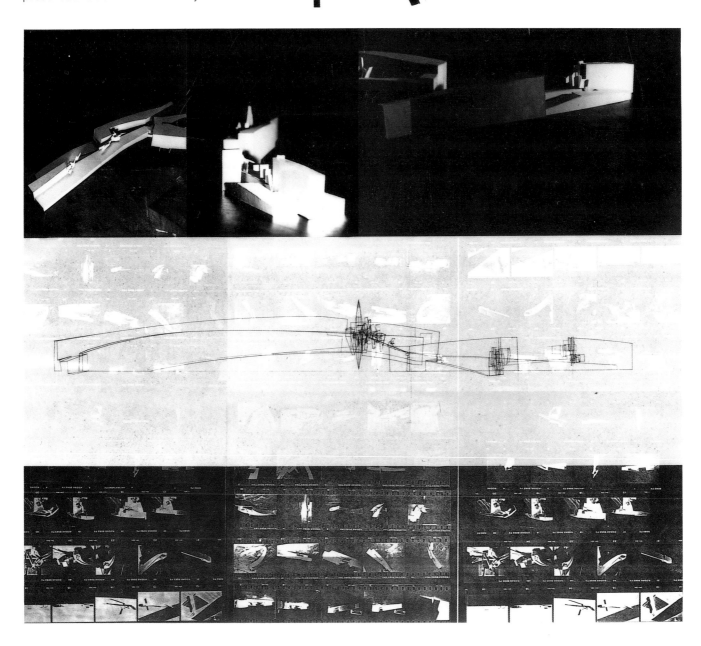

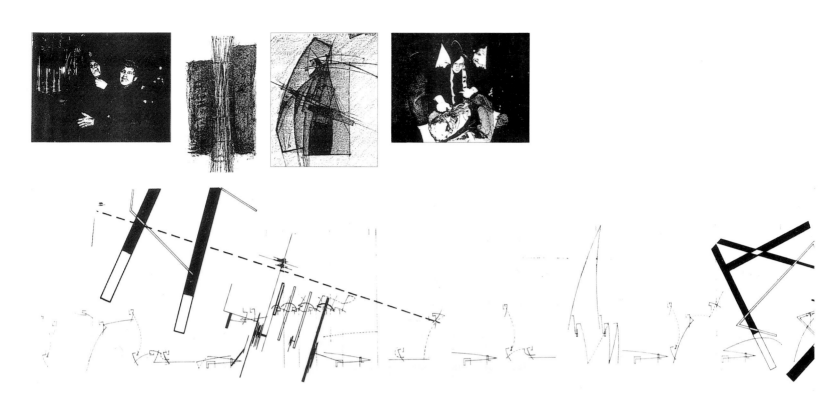

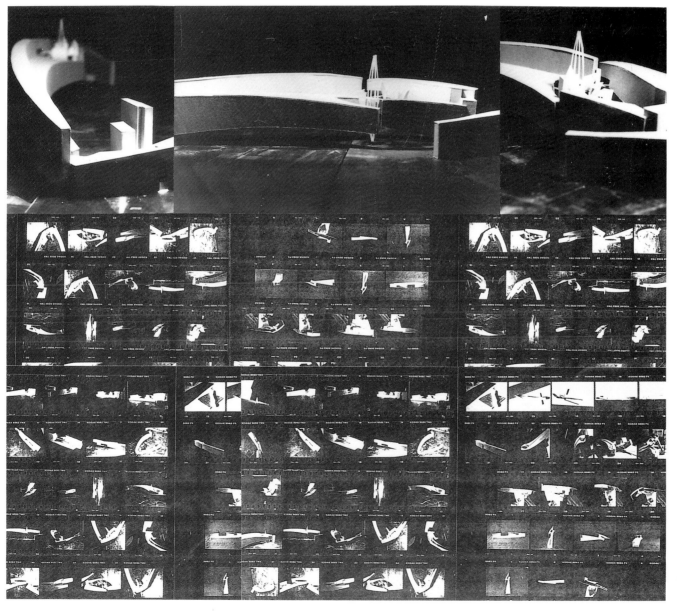

2nd PRIZE

JONATHAN BUCK
Polytechnic of Central
London, UK
Italie 13th Les Olympiades,
rue de Tolbiac

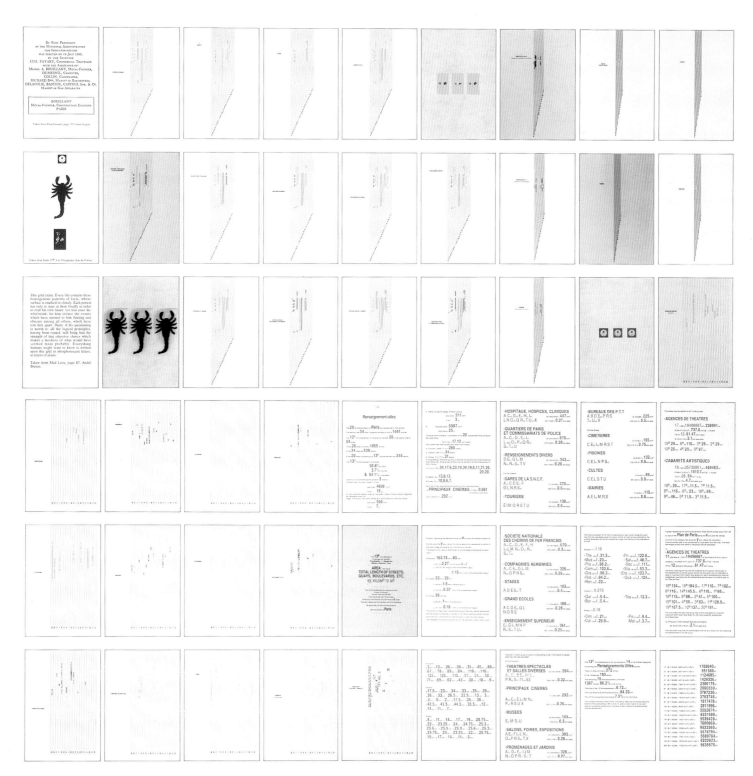

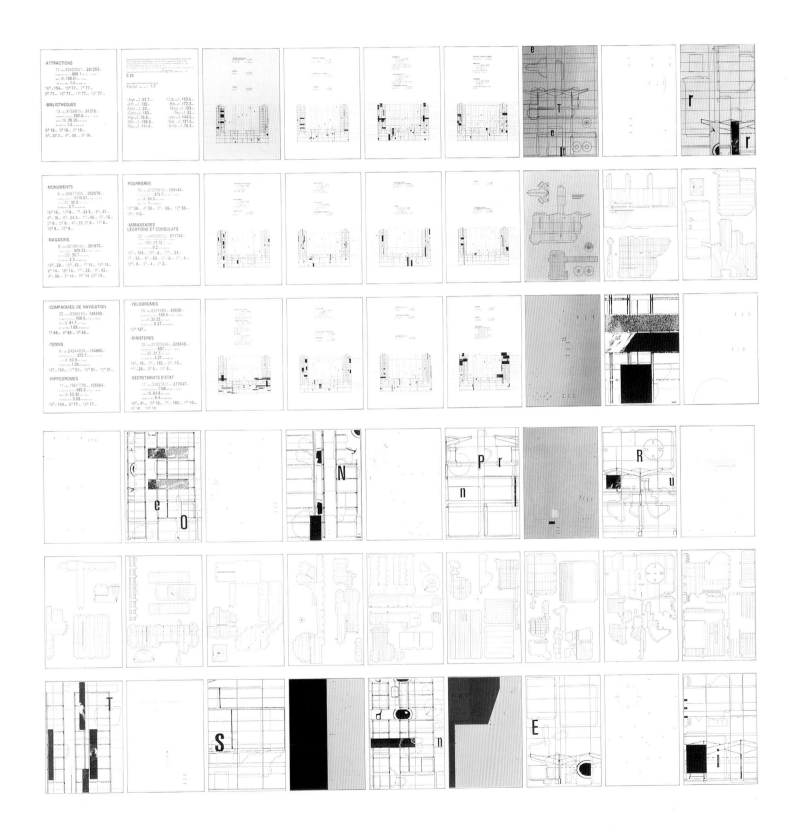

JOINT 3rd PRIZE

Nataliya Maximova, Dilara Zinatulina, Svetlana Nasretdinova, Svetlana Rasuleva, Regional Design School, Bashkirsky Dom, Russia, assisted by Elina Barykina, Mariya Balahontseva, Ildar Baikov, Iliya Litvinov, Varvara Sokolova, Vera Semyonova, Tagir Galiev and Veronika Zykina
Sultana House

JOINT 3rd PRIZE

YOUNG J YOON
Pennsylvania State
University, USA
The Phoenix

COMMENDED

IGOR KEBEL
University of Ljubljana,
Slovenia
Nautilus

YUVAL GLUSKA
Cooper Union, USA

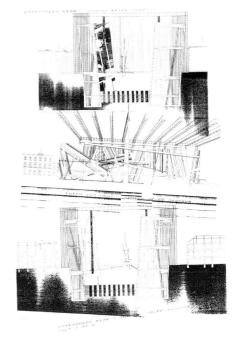

PATRICK J TIGHE AND
ROBERT YORK CROCKETT
UCLA Graduate School of
Architecture, USA
A Joycean Freeway Boyhood

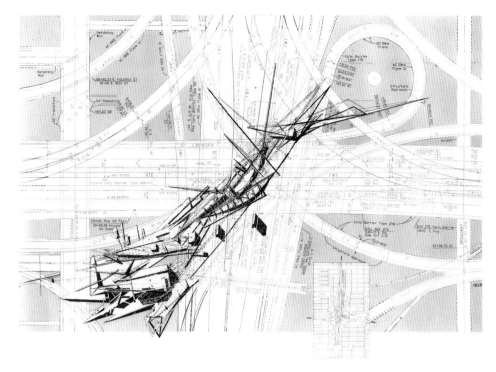

CATALIN MIHAI DRAGOMIR
Bartlett School of Architecture,
UK
Theories of Meaning

JUDGE

ITSUKO HASEGAWA
Busshoji Elementary School, Himi City, Japan

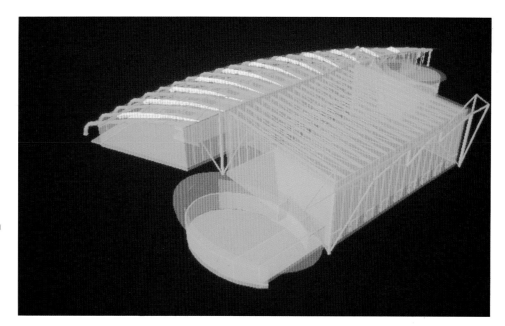

Busshoji Elementary School stands in a region of heavy snows. It is constructed as simple accommodation with one classroom per grade. The total number of students is about 120, a fairly small number which is expected to fall still further.

Ideally the aim is to create a space that establishes the perfect surroundings for primary education. The space should be fluid and flexible in structure, promoting the creativity of both the student and the teacher. It should not be constrained by a concept that emphasises any predetermined functional distribution. Based on this understanding, four blocks are established. The club house, open to parents and siblings, is part of a joint structure with the gymnasium, and the school building is complete with music room; a square has been placed between the gymnasium and school building.

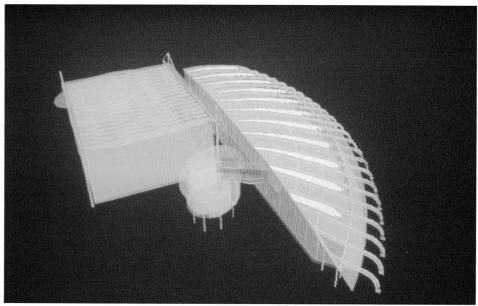

The basic theme of the design of the school building is that of a simple shelter characterised by great smoothness. It should harmonise with the changes in the natural environment and gently envelop the children with its rich sensitivities. The architecture fosters a soft, technological shelter-like appearance, resembling a seashell that allows you to hear the sounds of 'mother-waters'.

Busshoji Elementary School is a school on a hill. It blends in naturally with the surrounding environment, imparting an impression of a UFO comfortably landed on the hill. It is our desire that this elementary school becomes part of the hill through successful mutation.

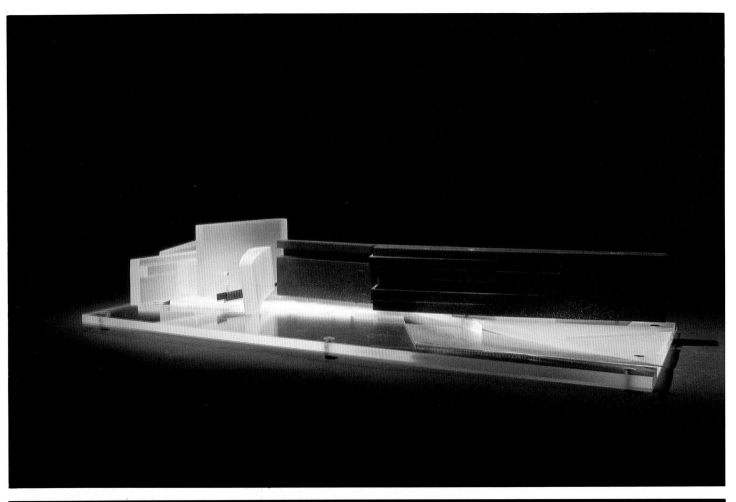

JUDGE
ZAHA HADID
Media Park, Zollhof 3

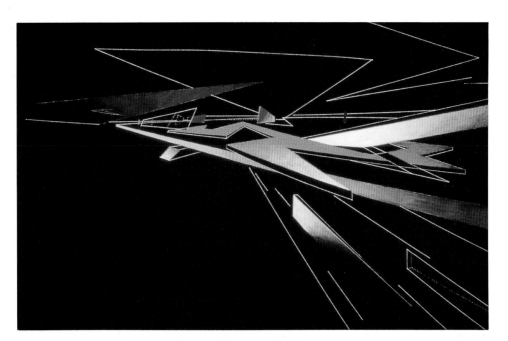

The development of the site is intended to be the impetus to the transformation of the old Dusseldorf Harbour into a new enterprise zone. So far, the potential of a new and generous urbanity relating to the scale of these former dockland areas has not been taken on.

The programme focuses on the accommodation of the communication business and creative professions, interspersed with shops, culture and leisure facilities. A strategy had to be devised that would be exemplary for the whole harbour area.

The distinctive quality of the area is its relationship to the river. The water edge is looked at as the active part of the site, animated with sport and other leisure activities. For these we propose an artificial modulated landscape which is protected from the street traffic by a building which functions as a wall. Special activities are highlighted against the continuous datum of the wall which accommodates all the studios and offices. At ground level are the more public-related businesses (galleries and showrooms) and above, those which require more tranquillity. Its street side is plain, while on the waterside the surface is open, partly articulated in relief, to allow for different floor depths. Where there is the need to separate a greater unit and express a certain corporate identity, then a section of the wall breaks free. The advertising agency, which breaks into a whole series of slabs, is also read as part of the wall. This cluster of slabs generates a variety of different spatial conditions inside. Where the slabs intersect a big space is carved out for conferences. Individually, the slabs provide well lit and well ventilated spaces for each department. The entrance lobby is at the point of intersection. The executive offices are double-height spaces on the side facing the water.

The ground behind the wall accommodates most of the public facilities and underneath the advertising agency are deep spaces for technical studios. A big triangular plane cuts the site, sloping against the wall and piercing through it underneath to form another entrance to the street. From here the shops are accessible.

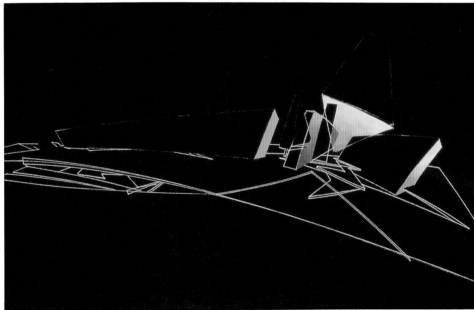

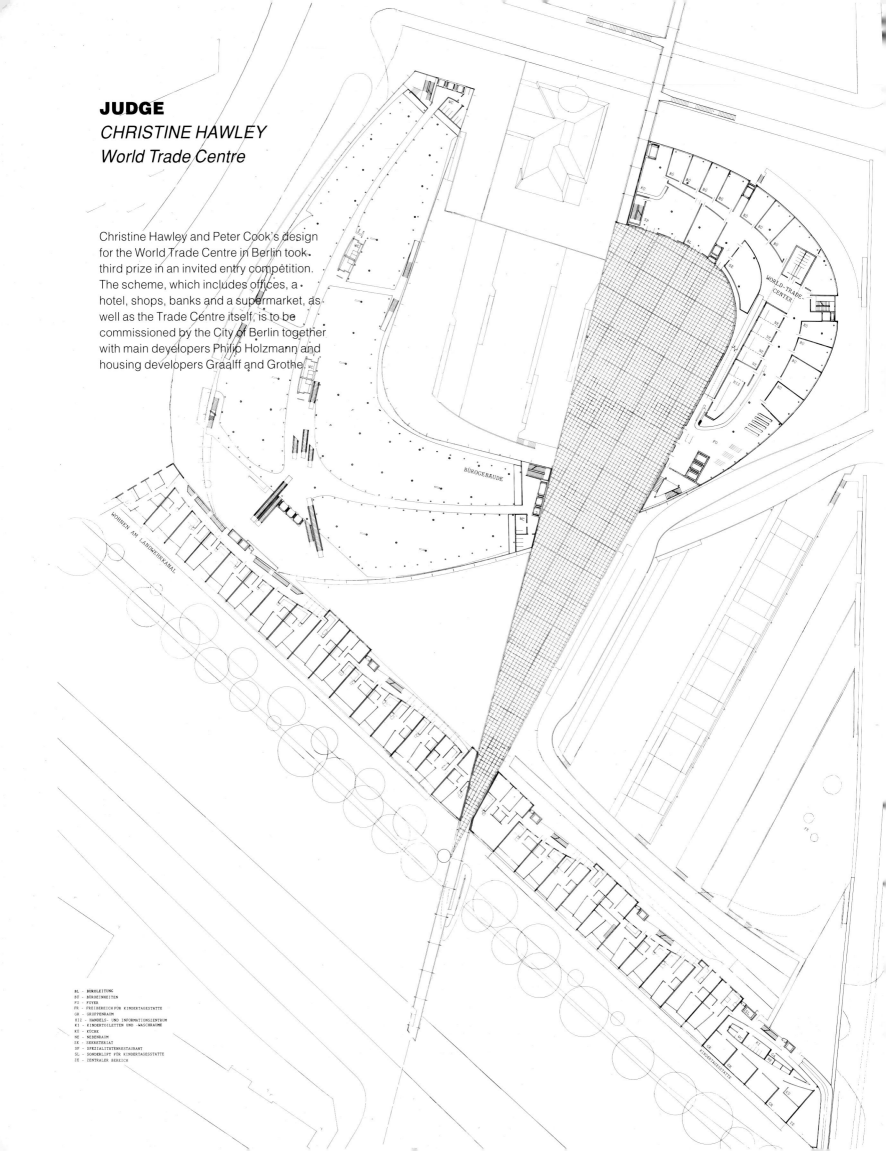

JUDGE
CHRISTINE HAWLEY
World Trade Centre

Christine Hawley and Peter Cook's design
for the World Trade Centre in Berlin took
third prize in an invited entry competition.
The scheme, which includes offices, a
hotel, shops, banks and a supermarket, as
well as the Trade Centre itself, is to be
commissioned by the City of Berlin together
with main developers Philip Holzmann and
housing developers Graalff and Grothe.

BL - BÜROLEITUNG
BÜ - BÜROEINHEITEN
FO - FOYER
FR - FREIBEREICH FÜR KINDERTAGESSTÄTTE
GR - GRUPPENRAUM
HIZ - HANDELS- UND INFORMATIONSZENTRUM
KI - KINDERTOILETTEN UND -WASCHRÄUME
KÜ - KÜCHE
NE - NEBENRAUM
SE - SEKRETARIAT
SP - SPEZIALITÄTENRESTAURANT
SL - SONDERLIFT FÜR KINDERTAGESSTÄTTE
ZE - ZENTRALER BEREICH